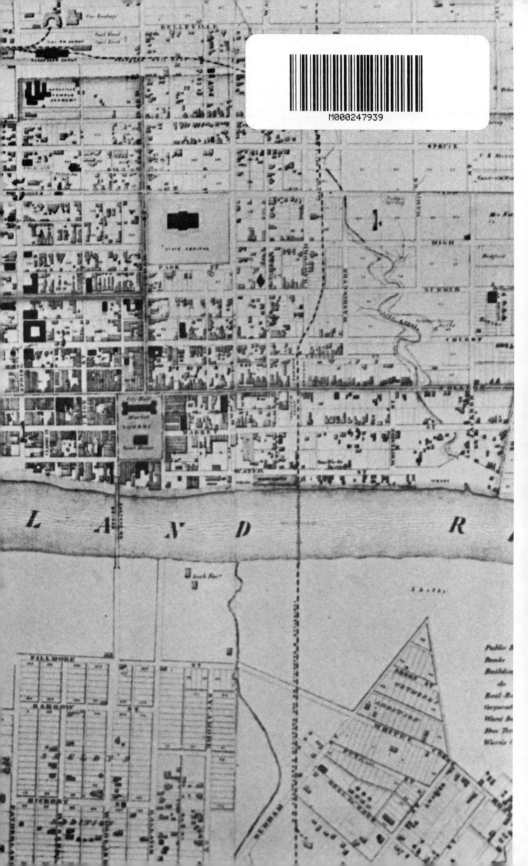

CHOSEN EXILE

CHOSEN EXILE

The Life and Times of
Septima Sexta Middleton Rutledge
American Cultural Pioneer

by
Mary Bray Wheeler and Genon Hickerson Neblett

RUTLEDGE HILL PRESS
Nashville, Tennessee

Combined Middleton/Rutledge crest
used by permission of families.

Library of Congress Cataloging in Publication Data

Wheeler, Mary Bray, 1942-
    Chosen exile.

    Bibliography: p.
    Includes index.
        1. Rutledge, Septima Sexta Middleton, 1783- 2. Nashville—
Biography. 3. Franklin Co., Tenn.—Biography. I. Neblett, Genon
Hickerson, 1923- joint author. II. Title.

F444.N253R878   976.8'55   80-14555

Published in Nashville, Tennessee, by Rutledge Hill Press,
Inc., 211 Seventh Avenue North, Nashville, Tennessee 37219.

Printed in the United States of America

Rutledge Hill Press gratefully acknowledges the assistance of
The Rutledge Company, Gadsden, Alabama.

Third printing, 1994

To

our "Family of the Heart;" those
descendants of Septima and Henry
whose lives have touched ours either
through the legacy of memory or the
gift of the present,

and to

Eugenia Price

whose writing inspired us,
whose advice encouraged us, and
whose faith helped keep ours strong.

Contents

Illustrations

Illustrations (continued)

Part IV

Part V

Illustrations (continued)

Part VI

Epilogue

End Sheet

Haydon Booth map (1860)
of Nashville, Tennessee, showing
Rutledge property near
University of Nashville.

Acknowledgements

Our strongest encouragement came from those people who offered advice, answered questions, and then continued to support us and believe in the value of our efforts. We extend grateful acknowledgement to the following:

For editorial assistance; Eugenia Price, Sandra J. Warden, James A. Hoobler, and Paul Meloun.

For publishing information; Oliver and Margaret Ikenberry, Bruce Nygren, Wendy Ragan, Larry Stone, Bradley Whitfield, and Stewart Williams.

For resourcing and study materials; Sophie Crane, Sara Daves, Margaret Hogshead, Evelyn O'Lee, Gladys Richter, Ruth Sims, Edythe Rucker Whitley, and Doug Williams.

For geological information and pottery dating; John Parks.

For photography; Charles N. Bayless, Ray Neblett, R. Alan Powell, Leslie Pritikin, Louis Schwartz, and Jim Wheeler.

For typing; Kathy J. Hansen, Margaret Hogshead, and Marcella Lawley.

Permission to print the following quotations has kindly been granted by: Ladies' Hermitage Association, inscription in *The Mourner Comforted*–Mary Middleton Rutledge Fogg to Andrew Jackson (1829); Middleton Place foundation, *Edward Rutledge, Signer of Declaration of Independence* (notes 4-4-78), RMI to Henrietta Draton [sic] (1798); Historical Society of Pennsylvania, short excerpts from the J. Francis Fisher Section–Cadwalader Collection–Mary Helen Hering Middleton to Septima Sexta Middleton Rutledge (Nov. 25, 1820; Aug. 25, 1821; Oct. 12, 1821; April 27, 1822; May 1823; Feb. 2, 1824; May 11, 1828; Dec. 31, 1828); Septima Sexta Middleton Rutledge to Mary Helen Hering Middleton (Sept. 18, 1838; Dec. 22, 1838; Oct. 28, 1847); Eliza Fisher to Henry Middleton (Jan. 1838); Rutledge Papers–Dreer Collection, John Randolph to Henry Rutledge (March 5, 1791); A. Jackson to Mary R. Fogg (Jan. 17, 1829) published in the Pennsylvania Magazine of History and Biography [Vol. XXV No. 100, Jan. 1902]; Mary Stevenson Poling and Eleanor Stevenson Rutledge, *Septima Sexta Middleton Rutledge* by Sabina Swope Forney Stevenson; *South Carolina Historical Magazine,* "Edward Rutledge to His Son, August 2, 1796" by Marvin Zahniser appearing in *SCHM* 64, April 1963, pp. 65-72 (short excerpts); South Carolina Historical Society,

Henry Rutledge to Henry Izard (1807); Mary Rutledge to Henry Rutledge (Aug. 22, 1808); Charles Cotesworth Pinckney to Henry Middleton Rutledge (Feb. 15, 1812); South Caroliniana Library. University of South Carolina, short excerpts from the Manigault Family Papers (1750-1898)—Mary Stead Pinckney to Mrs. Manigault; Edward Rutledge to his daughter Sally (Oct. 8, 1792); Mrs. Benjamin Bosworth Smith, *The Dream* by Katherine Felder Stewart (Aug. 15, 1977); Tennessee Historical Society, John Rutledge to Edward Rutledge (July 30, 1769). Other quotations are within the one hundred word limit or are within the public domain. Acknowledgements for the illustrations used appear with the individual photographs and permission to reproduce them is greatly appreciated.

Special thanks goes to Faith Hickerson Dycus, our enthusiastic, patient traveling companion; to Saye Bray Fleming, who became just as involved as Faith with our adopted family; and to Mary's mother, Frances Dority Bray, who made copies of the early manuscripts and loved Septima from the beginning. Much appreciation goes to Tom Dority, S. L. and Betsy Dority Collins, Rebie Harper, David and Leann Hickerson, and Tracy and Ann Hamilton Jackson for their faithful encouragement. Thanks goes to Diane Huizenga for helping make the Wheeler household operate smoothly in the midst of manuscripts and galleys, and to Marilisa, Jimmy, and Shannon Bray Wheeler for their cooperation and loyal sense of adventure. Grateful thanks goes especially to Ray Neblett for his steady, supportive interest throughout the years of research and writing involved in making this biography a reality.

No word of acknowledgement would be complete without an expression of gratitude to the Daugette family in Gadsden, Alabama. They have given us encouragement to continue our work and have followed our progress with enthusiasm. Staffing and resourcing were made available to us by Colonel Clarence W. Daugette, Jr., founder and president of Life Insurance Company of Alabama and president of the First National Bank of Jacksonville, Jacksonville, Alabama. His executive secretary, Marcella Lawley, worked with speed, diligence, and patient devotion to transform notebooks, pasteups, scribbled markings, index cards, and whole paragraphs by telephone into a smooth, typed manuscript.

Other individual acknowledgements appear in the Epilogue and under Resources. To Colonel Daugette, Marcella Lawley, Bradley and Sara Whitfield, our families, and each and every person who assisted us and shared in making *Chosen Exile* possible—we thank you.

Mary Wheeler and Genon Neblett
February, 1980

CHOSEN EXILE

Prologue

The forecasters said Friday August 17, 1979 would be a perfect day for the Nashville, Tennessee, area. It was just like any other beautiful August morning for most of the city, but for those occupants of a brown Cadillac with Alabama license tags, which slowed to a stop at the corner of Rutledge and Lea streets, the day was filled with magic. There, seventh and eighth generation descendants of Arthur Middleton and Edward Rutledge (South Carolina signers of the Declaration of Independence) would view the portion of the Henry Rutledge house, Rose Hill, which remains today.

The Nashville Tour Guides and local preservation societies call it "Historic Rutledge Hill." Very few visitors have known why this area, near the site of the old University of Nashville, carries the name Rutledge.

The country's Bicentennial celebration in 1976, as well as Nashville's plans for entering its third century in fall 1979, spring 1980, accelerated interest in local history.

The authors of this biography began in 1975 with an instinctive curiosity about Septima and Henry Rutledge and their motivation for joining the westward movement near the beginning of the nineteenth century. There were more questions than answers—by August of 1977, Middleton and Rutledge had become household words for the authors' families. "Historic Rutledge Hill," the old City Cemetery, and the Tennessee State Library and Archives soon became the most likely spots to locate the determined researchers.

The intrigue with the cultural impact that the Rutledge family had on the frontier city of Nashville encouraged descendants to make the pilgrimage to see for themselves, the locations of Chilhowee and Rose Hill, where it all began.

Visiting from Gadsden, Alabama, Colonel Clarence W. Daugette, Jr., his wife Florence, their son Clarence III, and their daughter Burt Lowe, listened with rapt attention to the description of the magnificent home of Col. Daugette's great-great-grandparents, Henry and Septima Rutledge.

The view of Nashville's modern skyline served to accent the wonder of that moment when each one, in his or her own imagination, claimed a part of the past. An 1860 map of the area, which included the Rutledge mansion, helped them visualize the trellised rose gardens which had graced the hillside and sloped to the banks of the Cumberland River.

The party traveled south on Fourth Avenue (originally Cherry Street), to the old City Cemetery for a visit to the Rutledge family plot. There was excited chatter accompanied by questions. Finally a quiet aura, almost a silent reverence, settled on the six. There was the rustle of paper, a text, a crisp voice reading a description of a ride from Rose Hill to the Cemetery. The character depicted was eighty-year-old Septima Sexta Middleton Rutledge, during the occupation of Nashville, by Union troops, in the winter of 1864. The authors shared their interpretation of how Septima may have felt as she contemplated her life.

> There is a certain peace which comes, a resolute kind of strength which God almighty bestows on the aging spirit . . . . Slowly a smile smoothed her wrinkled face and she longed to reach Heaven's windows—there at last she could look out on Charleston, Middleton Place, Janesse, her precious Chilhowee, and even Rose Hill and see each part of her life as if it were indeed for the very first time . . . . She thought how often she and Henry had referred to Chilhowee and Tennessee as their exile from home. They had chosen to remain and now this was their home.
>
> Septima placed her gloved hand on the granite stone marking the spot where she would be placed beside the one she had cherished for so long. She gently whispered, "Soon, very soon, I'll join you, Henry Middleton Rutledge, in our glorious new home—our final and most beloved exile."

The harsh conflicts of American history itself provide the background for this biography; it is a story of life which attempts to make the archives breathe, the family portraits speak, the letters and journals inspire as well as inform, the tombstones and brick foundations disclose the truth.

The story of Septima Sexta Middleton Rutledge brings into focus the life and times of an emerging nation: from colonial Charleston to frontier Nashville; from South Carolina low-country to Tennessee backwoods; from the American White House to the Russian courts of St. Petersburg; from colonies to states; from revolution to war between the states; from a harp's golden chord to the Indian's "singing river;" from home to exile.

Part I
SEPTIMA

(1783-1798)

1) Edward - The Oaks

2) Arthur

3)

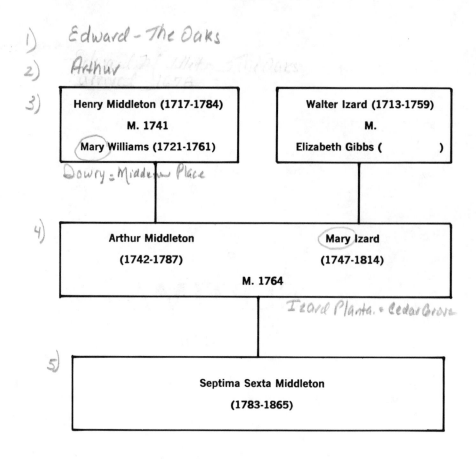

Henry Middleton (1717-1784)	Walter Izard (1713-1759)
M. 1741	M.
Mary Williams (1721-1761)	Elizabeth Gibbs ( )

Dowry = Middleton Place

4)

Arthur Middleton	Mary Izard
(1742-1787)	(1747-1814)
M. 1764	

Izard Planta. + Cedar Grove

5)

Septima Sexta Middleton
(1783-1865)

Genealogy I—Septima (1783-1798)

Chapter I

As Septima Middleton rode home with her mother and two sisters from St. Philip's Church, she was as happy as she ever had been. It was October 15, 1798, her fifteenth birthday. She wondered how she had ever contained her excitement long enough to listen to Reverend Frost. In fact her mind had not been on his message. Instead her thoughts had carried her from her home church in Charleston all the way to New York City.

As the carriage approached the Middleton house on East Bay, Septima recalled the exact wording of the announcement in the morning's *City Gazette*:

> Major Henry Rutledge, secretary to General Pinckney has arrived in N. Y. in the ship *Factor* from London.

Henry Middleton Rutledge. Septima couldn't remember a time when she hadn't thought well of him. In fact, she loved him. Now his father, Edward Rutledge, and her mother, Mary Middleton, had agreed on a marriage for Septima and Henry. This arranged marriage would be one born out of the young couple's respect for one another and a natural culmination of their friendship. It was a time in America's history when families became friends and friends became family.

1) Edward
2) Arthur
3) Henry
4) Arthur
5) Septima

The Middleton family line in America began with Edward Middleton who came to South Carolina by way of Barbados in 1678. His estate in the Parish of St. James, Goose Creek, comprised of many large land grants, was called The Oaks. He was Lords Proprietor deputy. His son Arthur Middleton was President of the 1719 Colonial convention which overthrew the Lords Proprietors. In 1739 Arthur's son Henry inherited vast land holdings in Carolina, Barbados, and England. It was in 1741 that Henry married Mary Williams, the only daughter and heiress of John Williams, a wealthy

Courtesy—Middleton Place Foundation

Flanking wings (1755) were detached from the main dwelling for fire protection. Library (right) and main house are now ruins. Gentlemen's guest wing (left) is today the surviving Middleton Place House.

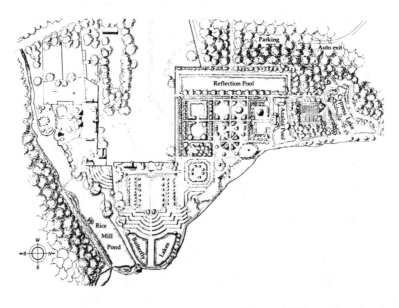

Courtesy—Middleton Place Foundation

Plan of Middleton Place

landowner, justice of the peace, and member of the South Carolina Assembly. Her dowry included an estate on the Ashley River, which together she and Henry named Middleton Place.

Built before 1741, the three-story main house resembled a stately Jacobean brick mansion. In 1755, Henry Middleton added two matching flanking wings; the south one for a gentlemen's guest wing, the north for a conservatory and twelve-thousand volume library.

Middleton Place became the setting for the first formal gardens in America. Over one hundred slaves worked for ten years to develop the grounds and landscape of patterned grandeur. In all the colonies there was none more magnificent. There was a sunken octagonal garden, which, shaded by the house, was the coolest location for summertime activities. Emerald terraces led to twin lakes that were perfectly formed to resemble open butterfly wings. One could walk past the flooded rice fields to the banks of the Ashley River and there lean against the giant Middleton Oak. Walking the grassy carpeted allées to the Reflection Pool and the Sundial Garden was indeed awesome in any season. The splendid shapes and geometrical designs were enhanced by the vivid splashes of color that rivaled the plumage of the native scarlet tanagers, wild parakeets, and orioles as they took flight over Middleton Place.

Henry Middleton made this his country seat from which he extended his political influence. He was Speaker of the Commons, Commissioner for Indian Affairs, and a member of the Governor's Council. He resigned the latter position in 1770 to become part of the leadership that opposed the British government. He was President of the Provincial Congress, and on October 22, 1774, was elected President of the First Continental Congress.

At that time the Honorable Henry Middleton owned fifty thousand acres of land and approximately eight hundred slaves. Following the death of his wife Mary Williams in 1761, he returned to his birthplace and childhood home, The Oaks. He gave Middleton Place to Arthur, the oldest of his five sons and seven daughters.

Arthur Middleton married Mary Izard in 1764, at which time they settled at Middleton Place. Arthur's political activities soon gained him recognition as a bold and radical revolutionary. He wrote political essays under the pen name Andrew Marvel. He succeeded his father in 1775 as an elected delegate to the Continental Congress, where he served with Thomas Heyward, Jr., Thomas

Portrait by Benjamin West,
—Middleton Place Foundation

Henry Middleton (1717-1784)

Courtesy—Middleton Place Foundation

**Portrait of Arthur Middleton (1742-1787) and Mary Izard Middleton
(1747-1814) and their son Henry (1770-1846) by Benjamin West,
London, 1771.**

Arthur Middleton died at age 45.

Arthur M / Martha L. R Contemporaries? Martha 15 yrs. older

Hopsewee?

Lynch, Jr., and his sister Henrietta's husband, Edward Rutledge.

On July 4, 1776, the South Carolina delegation joined the cause of independence by signing Thomas Jefferson's carefully worded document. Following the seige and occupation of Middleton Place and "Charles Town" by the British in 1780, Arthur Middleton and his brother-in-law, Edward Rutledge, along with other prominent men of Charles Town, were imprisoned on the ship Jersey and removed to the San Marco dungeon in St. Augustine, Florida. They were held captive for one year and finally exchanged in July, 1781, for British officers who were American prisoners of war. Arthur Middleton was immediately appointed to Congress in Philadelphia, then re-elected in June 1782. He finally returned to Middleton Place in 1783 where, it is recorded, he cheerfully engaged in restoring order, though his own losses were immense. He served in the South Carolina state legislature and was a trustee of Charleston College.

On October 15, 1783, Septima Sexta Middleton, his *seventh* child, *sixth* daughter (hence the Latin meaning of her name) was born at Middleton Place on the Ashley River.

Arthur and Mary Middleton had a son Henry, born September 28, 1770. The five daughters born before Septima were Maria Henrietta, August 13, 1772; Eliza Carolina, October 6, 1774; Emma Philadelphia, October 22, 1776; Anna Louisa, 1778; and Isabella Johannes, November 25, 1780. A second son, John Izard Middleton was born August 13, 1785.

On January 1, 1787, less than four years after Septima was born, Arthur Middleton died at the untimely age of forty-five. A son was born June 12, 1787, who died only ten days later.

At Arthur's death Middleton Place passed to his seventeen-year-old son Henry. Arthur's widow, Mary Izard Middleton, continued to divide her time between Middleton Place and Cedar Grove, the Izard estate which was now part of her vast holdings. She also leased the William Blake home on East Bay in Charleston for those dreaded fever months of summer which plagued the rice-growing plantation owners.

It is important to note that Septima Middleton was part of a family that placed great emphasis on classical education for girls. The Middleton women were tutored in language, literature, music—all areas of learning that would prepare them to be correct young ladies, well-endowed to take their proper places as mistresses of the great rice plantations.

Often at quite an early age the wife of a planter had the responsibility of overseeing the education and training of hundreds of slaves. Almost every planter of large means had his own carpenters, masons, blacksmiths, cabinet-makers, butchers, tailors, potters, waiters, as well as seamstresses, launderesses, pastry-cooks, trained nurses, and mid-wives. This was in addition to field workers and general household help. The instruction and welfare of the planter's "people" many times became the particular concern of his wife. Under her supervision many slaves were taught the English language.

South Carolina legislation made it *lawful* for any Negro to receive and profess the Christian faith and to be baptized. The larger plantations, such as Middleton Place, had a building designated as a school for the slaves and their children. It was not uncommon for slave families to gather around the front of the main house on Sunday afternoons to hear a message from the owner, to sing, to pray, and to recite the Scripture lessons they had learned at their own school-house.

Plantation life itself provided the necessary background for Mary Middleton to teach her daughters Maria, Eliza, Emma, Louisa,

Courtesy—Middleton Place Foundation

Aerial view showing geometric layout of Henry Middleton's garden carved out of the wilderness on the banks of the Ashley River.

Bell, and Septima the management skills they would need. They were prepared to assume positions of wealth or political influence. She expected them to become well acquainted with the arts, to develop a thorough knowledge of their religion, to accomplish expertise in fine sewing, articulate conversation, and generous hospitality. The Middleton girls were taught to ride side-saddle and probably joined their mother in her customary equestrian surveys of Middleton Place from the Izard plantation, Cedar Grove, across the Ashley River.

Musical talent was developed by a governess or tutor. Instruction included study on the pianoforte, the flute, and, for Septima, her fine golden Italian harp.

When Septima was eleven, an uprising in Santo Domingo in 1794 caused a great influx of distressed refugees to the United States. This prompted Charleston's St. Cecilia Society to sponsor benefit concerts where the music of Haydn, Corelli, and Grétry was performed. *321 East Bay .*

In like manner the Middleton home in Charleston became the scene of many private Wednesday evening musicals. These were most usually charitable events inspired by the talented Santo Domingans and community needs. Septima often played her harp and sang for the assembled guests, thus becoming quite a charming addition to these gatherings. The quality of these performances was greatly enhanced by the arrival from London of musical instruments sent by the American Ambassador Thomas Pinckney.

There are early references to Mary Middleton's compassion and concern for the sick. The year before Septima was born, August of 1782, twenty-four-year-old Gabriel Manigault, who had just returned from school in England, was stricken with the fever while visiting Middleton Place. He had spent the better part of a year visiting the different neighboring plantations to avoid capture by the British and had been there on the Ashley about a month. He wrote in his diary that Mrs. Mary Middleton cared for him during the intermittent and then continued bouts which placed him in such a "dangerous situation." He insisted that for his recovery he was "chiefly indebted to the care and attention" which he vowed to "ever remember with gratitude." He "remained there until the beginning of October following," and mentioned often the hospitality and concern shown him by Mary Middleton.

There are other references to Mary Middleton's attention to the needs of close frends and relatives during illness and the care given them by her and her daughter Septima. It is appropriate to assume that this mother and her youngest daughter maintained a relationship of concern for others which would influence Septima as she matured and assumed responsibilities of her own.

There is little primary information about Septima's childhood other than general references to the family and quality of life at Middleton Place. These sources, as well as the known customs and traditions of the South Carolina low-country plantations, convey the idea that arranging suitable marriages provided security and kept property within the family. Ties of blood as well as friendship were of utmost consideration. It was no surprise that, at age fifteen, Septima was betrothed to her first cousin, Henry Middleton Rutledge.

Courtesy—Citizens and Southern National Bank, Charleston, S.C.

321 East Bay, built before 1789 by William Blake. Acquired and restored in 1965 by Historic Charleston Foundation.

Arthur's widow, Septima's mother, leased this house.

Part II

HENRY

(1775-1798)

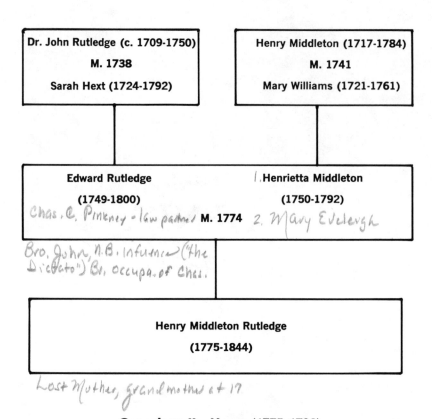

Dr. John Rutledge (c. 1709-1750)

M. 1738

Sarah Hext (1724-1792)

Henry Middleton (1717-1784)

M. 1741

Mary Williams (1721-1761)

Edward Rutledge

(1749-1800)

Chas. C. Pinkney - law partner M. 1774

1. Henrietta Middleton

(1750-1792)

2. Mary Eveleigh

Bro. John, N.B. Infuence ("the Dictato") Br, occupa. of Chas.

Henry Middleton Rutledge

(1775-1844)

Lost Mother, grandmother at 17

Genealogy II—Henry (1775-1798)

Chapter Two

Henry Middleton Rutledge was born in Charleston, South Carolina, April 5, 1775. His grandfather Dr. John Rutledge had immigrated to Carolina from County Tyrone, Ireland (Ulster), in 1735. His maternal grandfather was Henry Middleton of The Oaks and Middleton Place.

From the time Henry was five years old, things were not right in the Rutledge household. It was then that his younger brother, two-year-old Edward, Jr., was burned to death after toddling too close to the nursery fire. Henrietta Middleton Rutledge was never able to overcome her shock and grief at the loss of her child even when a daughter Sarah was born two years later. Henrietta's condition put serious limitations on her husband's political activities. Edward's career had been enhanced by his marriage to Arthur Middleton's sister in their early years together. However, following young Edward's tragic death, Henrietta suffered lapses of memory, deep depressions, and at times would lunge into the fire in an attempt to save the child she had lost. Her husband refused to leave her and resigned himself to work that kept him near home.

Even though Edward built quite a successful law practice with his brother-in-law Charles Cotesworth Pinckney, he longed to return to public service. His own ambitions were thrust upon Henry, who did not share his father's interest in politics.

Tragically, Henry's mother and his grandmother Sarah Hext Rutledge both died Sunday, April 22, 1792 only about two weeks after Henry's seventeenth birthday. Then on Wednesday, June 16, of the same year, his Aunt Elizabeth, wife of Edward's brother John, died suddenly.

On October 28, 1792, a few months following Henrietta's death, Edward married Mary Shubrick Eveleigh, the widow of Col. Nicholas Eveleigh who died April 16, 1791. Her brother, Thomas Shubrick, was Henry's closest friend in Charleston. Mary Rutledge became a peaceful influence on the entire family and always referred to Edward's children as though they were her own. With the improvement of their family stability, Edward's political activities resumed. His influence in South Carolina became stronger than ever, resulting in his being elected state senator in 1796 and governor in 1798.

His brother John, Edward's senior by ten years, suffered great depression after the death of his wife and his mother in 1792. By 1795 John Rutledge, the state's chief justice and South Carolina's first governor, was reduced to dwindling political influence. Arranging good marriages for the Rutledge children became more and more important if political power was to remain in the family.

Both Rutledge brothers had always been obsessed with matters of state. Their backgrounds, their devotion during the struggle for independence, were matters of record. John Rutledge had influenced his younger brother, Edward, from the beginning of his career.

A letter written to Edward by his brother John while Edward was studying at the Middle Temple in London was addressed from Charleston, July 30, 1769, and began:

> Dr Ned/
> As I had not leisure before you went to reduce to writing some Observations which I mentioned verbally to you concerning your studies in England, I take this first opportunity . . . of doing it lest you may forget any of 'em.

The very first page of this quite lengthy letter mentioned the importance of learning shorthand and recording *all* that he heard at the "Bar," and even for practice, everything he heard from the "pulpit." The letter continued:

> . . . But you must exert yourself to the utmost in being able by some means or other to attend the House of Commons constantly, or at least whenever any thing of consequence is to come on. . . . make yourself well acquainted with the Speakers—Reading Lectures upon Oratory will never make you an orator. . . . I wd also have you attend the House of Lords upon every occasion worth it— . . . I known nothing more entertaining, and likely to give you a graceful manner of speaking than seeing a good Play well acted— . . . You must not neglect the Classics, but rather go thro' 'em from beginning to end. I think you had better get a private tutor who will point out their Beauties to you . . . . I wd have you read occasionally the purest English Authors to acquire an elegant Style & Expression . . . . The History of England should be read with great care & attention, . . . Don't neglect to learn Surveying. That is the principal branch of Mathematics which you'll have occasion for . . . Stock yourself

with a good collection of Law Maxims, both Latin & English. They are of great use—don't omit any that you come across, . . .

I believe you will think I have cut out work enough for you while in England, & indeed tho' it is a long time to look forward if you mind your business you will have not too much time to spare. However I hope you will not fail to do this. Your own Reputation is at stake. You must either establish it when young or it will be very difficult to acquire it.—I am persuaded you need no Argument to urge you to it, & sh^d be most heartily vexed & disappointed if you do not answer my Expectations when you return.—

One word with regard to your Deportment:—Let your Dress be plain always, in the City— & elsewhere, except where it is necessary it sh^d be otherwise—& your behavior rather grave—remember the old man's advice to his son Think *twice* before you speak once. . . . I have no other motive but your welfare which I decidedly wish, & therefore I w^d not omit any thing in which there is a chance of being any ways useful to you. Farewell my d^r Brother. Let me hear from you by every opportunity, & believe me

> Yrs. Affec^tly
> J. Rutledge

It reads as though John were Edward's father rather than his older brother. The letter was quoted by Edward to his son Henry many times, especially when he was away at Columbia University.

War with England severely interrupted the traditional educational patterns in the American colonies. South Carolinians of political influence, particularly six of the eleven members of the state's first Provincial Congress, had been Middle Templars—Charles Cotesworth Pinckney, Charles Pinckney, Arthur Middleton, Thomas Lynch, Jr., Thomas Heyward, Jr., and John Rutledge. All four signers of the Declaration of Independence from South Carolina studied at the Middle Temple in London. Missing for Henry was the experience of studying at Middle Temple and the prestige involved in being admitted to the English bar. This family responsibility to maintain position was so important to both John and Edward that Henry feared no matter what he did he would never quite please either of them. Even as late as 1796, Henry was aware that most of his father's decisions in the state senate were made in consultation with Uncle John. "Dictator" was the right name for his uncle.

During the British occupation of Charleston, Governor John

Photo—Photo Designers, Gadsden, Al.
Oil painting by Annie Rowan Forney Daugette
of an original portrait by Earle.
Courtesy—Estate of Annie Rowan
Forney Daugette

Edward Rutledge (1749-1800)

JOHN RUTLEDGE.
Nat-1739 - Ob-1800

Courtesy—Tennessee Historical Society

Charles Cotesworth Pinckney
(1746-1825)

Courtesy—Tennessee Historical Society

John Rutledge (1739-1800)
" Dictator "

Rutledge, narrowly escaping capture, carried South Carolina's most important papers in his own carriage to a position of safety in North Carolina. Total power was bestowed on him by the state legislature only hours before the fall of his native city. It was well known that the government of South Carolina resided in the carriage of John Rutledge. His political control was absolute, and soon South Carolina's governor came to be known simply as "Dictator John."

Henry wanted somehow to be his own person, separate from his father and his uncle John. He really enjoyed forensics—he read the law especially well—yet somehow he didn't possess the famous Rutledge fervor for political life. _Manhattan?_

Henry's years at Columbia University in New York were of great intellectual stimulus. Though only fourteen years old, he was introduced to the classics through a series of tutors. At that time, he became acquainted with a young Virginian, John Randolph, who after 1810 called himself John Randolph of Roanoke. Henry and John studied privately with Professor Cochrane of Columbia

Courtesy—South Carolina Historical Society

117 Broad Street, Post Revolution home of Edward Rutledge (1749-1800), Charleston, South Carolina

Septima's father in laws' home

with whom they read Demosthenes. This part of their education was all too brief. Randolph at sixteen and Rutledge at fourteen had been restless, eager to experience the present rather than study the past.

John Randolph was such a racing enthusiast that his friendship with Henry soon began to take them both away from their study of the law. He once visited Henry, making the trip to Charleston on horseback. The gawky, yellow-haired young man actually rode the life out of his steed. Such daring disregard for consequences may have impressed some, but Edward Rutledge made it clear to this impudent, self-possessed friend of Henry's that he considered him a bad influence.

John Randolph was certainly different. His moods ran the gamut of emotion. One thing for sure—he expected Henry to correspond frequently and was subject to pouting if the letters from him weren't personal, gossip-filled, and exactly to his liking. He considered "Rutledge," as he was given to calling him, his very best companion, and yet Henry was never quite daring enough for John. In his younger days, horse racing and gambling had been no more than something to dabble in for Henry—for John Randolph they were obsessions.

In a letter to Henry at Columbia dated 25 March 1791 John Randolph referred to his love of racing in a subtle way:

> . . . Everything goes on in the old Track, with regard to my pursuits.

Then he admonished Henry for not writing:

> You well know what pleasure your letters afford me; why then will you withold [sic] them from your friend?—I shall be very laconic, because I begin to grow dull and tedious—Protestations, I conceive, useless to convince you of the purity of my Friendship —Adieu!

Their correspondence continued despite long absences, as did their friendship.

The children of Edward Rutledge were much influenced by the Pinckney families. His daughter Sarah was ten years old when she accompanied the Thomas Pinckneys to Europe in 1792. She left with them following the death of her mother. She attended the finest schools—among them, Madame Campan's in Paris. Thomas Pinckney, brother of Charles Cotesworth, was minister plenipotentiary to England and later to Spain, positions which gave him the opportunity of providing these cultural advantages for Sarah.

Edward wrote to Sally, as they called her, in October of 1792:

> You cannot imagine my dearest Daughter, how delighted I was to receive your very affectionate letter of the 7th of August. I felt uncommon Pleasure, to find that, the Passage, of my dear little Angel, had on the whole, been so agreeable. . . . You must consider yourself, as more, than commonly fortunate, in being placed under the care of those who have taken the charge of you. You must never forget, that their Friendship, and affection for us, are their only Inducements. And you must continue to remember, that my Pleasure and indeed my Happiness, will be increased, or lessened, by the accounts which I shall receive, from them, for you—I will now take Leave of this Subject by saying, that I have neither Fears or Doubts about it: but that I am satisfied, in my own Mind, you will give me no occasion to be sorrowful—

Edward continued with some advice about thank-you notes and manners and then closed with a word about Henry:

> I hear frequently from your Brother, who is well; & is now pursuing his Studies at New York. The Court is now sitting & I must quit— All your Friends give their Love to you—God bless you my dearest Daughter, & believe me your most affectionate Father—
>
> Ed. Rutledge

Following Henry's studies in New York he traveled to London and stayed with his sister Sally and the Thomas Pinckney family. He later served as secretary to his uncle Charles Cotesworth Pinckney and the American legation to France. Charles Cotesworth, like Edward, had married a sister of Arthur Middleton, Sarah, who died on May 8, 1784. Besides being brothers-in-law, Charles Cotesworth Pinckney and Edward Rutledge were law partners. It was only natural that Pinckney would choose his favorite nephew to accompany him to France. Thomas and Charles Cotesworth Pinckney, had gained much prominence through appointments from President George Washington, so that, in 1796, when Charles Cotesworth was asked by Washington to head the United States legation to France, he chose Henry as his secretary.

Owned by Burwell Marshall Hardy,
Louisville, Ky.
Courtesy—Benjamin Bosworth Smith,
Charleston, S.C.
Photo—Jim Wheeler

**Henry Middleton Rutledge
(1775-1844) Miniature
painted c. 1796-1800,
artist unknown**

Edward Rutledge wrote to his son in London to encourage him to join his Uncle Pinckney in the mission to France.

August 2, 1796

My dearest Henry,

I wrote you on the 30th. ult. informing you of your Uncle Pinckney's appointment to a place of honorable importance in Europe, acquainting you to hold yourself in readiness to join him on the first summons, and hinting that your presence would be required. He will be himself the bearer of this letter, and will deliver it with his own hands, I shall therefore write you without restraint.

The President having judged it absolutely necessary to recall Mr. Monroe from France, and send some person to that Republic, in whom he could confide and to whom no objection could be taken by either of the parties which unhappily divide the States, wrote to your Uncle Pinckney a very full letter on the occasion, urging him by the love which he bore his Country, and by the regard he had for her safety, to dedicate himself to her service; and stating the situation of things to be such, as left him in my opinion without a reasonable excuse. As soon as he received the letter, he placed it in my hands; we viewed the affair in various points; and altho it was manifest that he would make a considerable sacrifice of professional emolument and would hazard the malice of his enemies, and part with a portion of his own tranquility, by an acceptance of the appointment; yet if there were occasions and seasons, in which all private considerations, were to yield to public good, the present hour required that he should not view himself in the light of an individual. Such being the result of our reflections, he wrote to the President, notifying his acceptance, and sent off his dispatches by two different conveyances. I saw him the next day, and in making his arrangements his mind turned itself towards you. It is not necessary to repeat every thing he said in favor of one who is generally known to possess a large share of his affection; he however expressed a wish to have you near him, said he should write for you the moment he landed; desired I would signify his intention to you; spake a good deal of the implicit confidence which should subsist between a Minister, and his private Secretary, and concluded by saying as he could place that confidence in you, he should make you his Secretary, if on further consideration he did not think, it would not be injurious to your interest. I saw him again the next Day; he told me he had decided the matter in his own Mind—that you must be his private Secretary—and that he would undertake to direct your legal Studies. Thus then Mr. Secretary, I give you joy of your appointment which is honorable in itself; made more so, by the manner in which it has been conferred and by the Minister with whom you are connected. . . .

Edward wanted to remind Henry of the family obligations involved and the responsibilities which accompanied privileges.

. . . you know as well as I do, that the profession of Law opens the way in America, to the most important Offices in the Union: and altho' I am fully convinced you are neither anxious, or desirous of entering on public duties, yet at certain times and in certain seasons it is so absolutely incumbent on Men of talents, and independence, and virtue, to participate in the affairs of the Republic, that I consider your chance for retirement to be small indeed. The family my Son from which you have descended; the style of your education; the long and steady attachment of your uncle Pinckney towards you; the early acquaintance which you have formed with public men; the habits to which they themselves are accustomed of considering your nearest connections, as the property of their Country form such a

Henry Rutledge became personal Sec. to his Uncle Chas. C. Pinckney as head legation to France

26   CHOSEN EXILE

combination of circumstances as forbid the idea of private Life. Look my Son, into the bosom of America, and you will soon become sensible, that she will be exposed to many rude attacks within, as well as from without, many sharp conflicts, and many convulsive struggles. She is not alone the asylum of the virtuous, she is also the receptacle of the wicked—like the beams of the heavenly Luminary, she shines upon the unjust, as well as the just. The constant migrations from every part of Europe, has given her an unnatural population, and from the conflicts which will be the Offspring of these opposite passions, many and serious evils may be expected to arise. In such a state of things, it will be incumbent on the descendants of those, to whom America is indebted for her Independence to vindicate the rights of their Country and maintain them with as sacred a piety, as they would the reputation of their ancestors. . . .

Edward continued for several paragraphs with advice he thought well for Henry to heed. Some of his words and phrases were the result of his brother John's influence, and were reminiscent of the letter "Dictator John" had written Edward some twenty-seven years ago. Henry was now twenty-one and would benefit from this passing on of invaluable knowledge from one generation to the next. His father and uncle had shown concern for him and his education—their words about learning and conduct were ageless. Edward cautioned Henry:

Hear every thing—learn every thing—reflect on every thing—combine every thing—combine them with the persons from whom they came—the occasion which gave rise to them; and the circumstances which attend them—. . . . take minutes of all *important* conversations; in the line of your Office, take minutes of *all* conversations, for they may become important. Study the characters of all diplomatic Men from the different nations, as far as opportunities occur, particularly from those nations, with which we are or probably may be connected; mark the fort, and the foible of each—and in a word 'avail yourself of your situation.'

Henry really had little choice but to follow his father's advice and join the American legation to France. He traveled from London to Paris early in December of 1796. He was there when Charles Cotesworth, his wife Mary, and young daughter Eliza arrived on the evening of December 5. Henry and his uncle Pinckney began their duties the next morning by giving James Monroe their official letters from American Secretary of State Rufus King and his release from duty. Monroe tried to be friendly and helpful despite his bitterness over his abrupt recall by Washington.

The Pinckneys leased a five-room apartment at the Hotel des Tuileries, Rue St. Honoré. Henry stayed with them. There was some uneasiness as to how Charles Delacroix, the French minister of foreign relations, would receive the new delegation.

Monroe sent Delacroix a note stating that Pinckney was ready to present his official letters to the Directory. On December 9 Delacroix informed Monroe that he would see the two ministers from America. He greeted Monroe, Pinckney, and young Rutledge with "great stiffness," then seemed to relax the formality and promised to send them the necessary permits for their stay in France. No one could remain in Paris without proper credentials. Henry and his uncle Pinckney returned to their apartment feeling they would be immune from arrest and that their acceptance was assured.

Three days passed with no word from Delacroix. On December 12, Pinckney learned that there would be no cards—no permits—no safety for their mission. The decision of the Directory was:

> that it will no longer recognize nor receive a minister plenipotentiary from the United States, until after a reparation of the grievances demanded of the American government, and which the French republic has a right to expect.

Henry delivered a note of reply from Pinckney to Delacroix on December 13 which asked for an effort to resolve points of difference saying that he had come to France to negotiate in good faith. All of this was in vain. Unknown to Charles Cotesworth and Henry there had been undated instructions, announcing the suspension of normal diplomatic relations between France and the United States. These orders had been sent to Delacroix, before the Americans arrived, by Pierre Auguste Adet, the French minister to the United States.

Charles Cotesworth was not only angry but alarmed that the minister of the *police générale* could have them thrown into jail as strangers just because Delacroix would not give them official recognition. Pinckney knew that the Directory wanted to force them to leave France, to abandon his responsibility, and that he must wait for written orders. The communication expelling them came late in January, 1797. On February 5, they left for Amsterdam to wait for instructions from the American government.

News of the rejection of Pinckney by the French Directory reached Philadelphia a few days after John Adams became the second president of the United States. Adams responded quickly by appointing ministers from three different areas, Charles Cotesworth Pinckney of South Carolina, John Marshall of Virginia, and Elbridge Gerry of Massachusetts, in an effort to unite the country on foreign policy. Pinckney, Marshall, and Gerry were commissioned on May 31, 1797, to negotiate a treaty of amity with France. Henry Rutledge was to serve as secretary for this second Pinckney mission. In the year that followed, Henry experienced the advantages and disadvantages of public service in a foreign country.

Henry was content with his work. He had no overwhelming responsibilities, no policy-making duties. His work involved keeping accurate records and maintaining correspondence. He was careful to do what his father had asked, and at every opportunity he pursued a thorough study of the law. Uncle Pinckney was an exacting teacher. No single professor at Columbia had demanded so much concentration. Henry developed a determined attitude toward his work, yet still he was not able to muster a love for the political arena. He may well have doubted his ability to ever measure up to Edward and John Rutledge and the ambitious fervor they had expected of him. His commission in the army and the rank of Major were a part of his appointment to the legation. He must have enjoyed his official position and the social entry afforded him.

Correspondence while in Paris from Mary Stead Pinckney, second wife of Charles Cotesworth Pinckney, to Mrs. Gabriel Manigault back home in Charleston, hinted at the popularity experienced by the handsome twenty-two-year-old, gray-eyed Major Henry Middleton Rutledge in French society. In one of her letters, following a performance of Mozart's *The Marriage of Figaro,* she reported:

> Henry was at the Opera again last night with *that woman.* She had her hind hair drawn high, a muslin dress, gauze drawers and no petticoats.

Henry's name was linked also with that of a Mme Tallieu of Paris, and Eleanor Hering, sister of Mary Helen Hering, wife of Henry Middleton of Middleton Place. Mary Pinckney related the gossip in her letters and indicated that although Henry had close association with Mary Helen and Henry Middleton while in

London, he had never even been introduced to Eleanor nor had he visited the Hering ancestral home, Heybridge Hall in Bath, England. Henry's status as an eligible bachelor must have been quite a challenge for the Embassy wives in London and Paris.

There was yet another story concerning the love life of Henry Rutledge of South Carolina. There was a mysterious beautiful young countess. Family tradition concerning the countess comes through a great-granddaughter who records that:

> She returned his love and they were to be married, but she had been betrothed when a child to a titled Frenchman, who would not release her. So poor great-grandfather came back to America and married his first cousin, Septima Middleton. They lived very happily together, but my mother used to say, "Grandmama was always a little jealous of the beautiful French countess."

Edward Rutledge informed his son Henry that he was to marry his cousin Septima Middleton soon after his return from France.

By April, 1798, Henry sensed his uncle Pinckney's uneasiness more each day. Somehow it seemed inevitable that they would be recalled to America. To Henry there seemed to be a general climate of misunderstanding between the people of France and America that should never have happened. The political problems that were the result of the rejection by France of the original Pinckney mission only escalated the growing bitterness at home. Attitudes toward France were hostile in America, particularly in South Carolina where Pinckney was known to be a friend of France. That country, that French Republic, had officially ignored, socially cast out, and even threatened to imprison this proud Charlestonian. Now he had returned, negotiations were attempted, there was more belligerence—even a bribe offering French goodwill for a price. The Pinckney temper surfaced. This trusted, fellow citizen wrote friends and relatives in Charleston telling of the humiliation he and the country suffered at the hands of the French Directory. Political allies of Charles Cotesworth and Thomas Pinckney, Henry, Edward, and John Rutledge were convinced now that the Federalist's firm treatment was necessary in dealings with republican France. The

Federalist camps of Washington and Adams had more support than ever from the South because the government was supportive of Pinckney. The mission in France may have failed, but political strategy at home was a success. Party allegiance was closely tied to foreign policy in this early national period. The infant America was sensitive to hostility, recognized moods of tyranny, and wanted no part of suppression.

In the late spring of 1798, President Adams reported to Congress the failure of the Commission to France and released the full correspondence between the American legation and Talleyrand's agents. He identified the three French agents Hottinguer, Bellamy, and Hauteval only as X, Y, and Z. Adams disclosed all the particulars of the suggested $240,000 to Talleyrand in return for certain concessions, including French respect for the American flag. Charles Cotesworth Pinckney refused the bribe and the American papers referred to the incident as the "XYZ affair."

Henry arrived in New York on the ship *Factor* from London in October, and upon deliverance of his official letters he departed for home. The Pinckney's were to spend Thanksgiving at Mount Vernon with George and Martha Washington. Henry declined the invitation as he had been gone from home close to three years. At twenty-three he was prepared to enter the legal profession as his father expected.

Edward Rutledge became governor of South Carolina in December of 1798, and plans for the marriage of his son Henry to Arthur Middleton's daughter Septima were completed. This marriage would once more unite two of the most prominent famlies in South Carolina. The names of Middleton and Rutledge, as well as Pinckney, were still synonomous with South Carolina and, indeed, with American political power, though it had been twenty years since the signing of the Declaration of Independence.

Part III
SEPTIMA AND HENRY

(1799-1815)

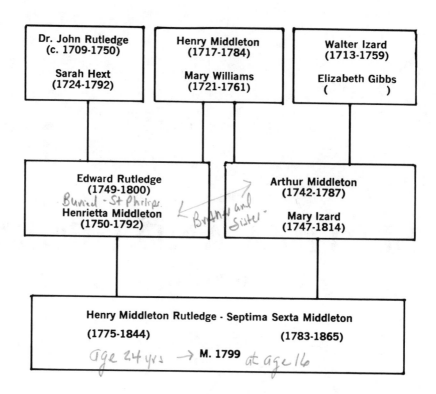

Genealogy III—Septima and Henry (1799-1815)

Chapter Three

The year 1799 was filled with excitement and anticipation for the Middleton and Rutledge famlies. Governor Edward Rutledge was most pleased at the prospect of his son's marrying one of Arthur Middleton's daughters. Political allies within the family strengthened party positions. Edward had benefitted greatly himself from his own marriage to Henrietta Middleton before her years of depression. His brother John had often reminded him of how much Edward's political career and legal practice had been guided and shaped by that marital link with Arthur Middleton's sister. Edward believed that with Septima to steer him Henry would be better equipped to assume his place in the political arena.

Edward's health was failing, and it was all he could do to manage his duties as governor. He leaned more and more on Henry to help him. Henry's uncle John was taken to long periods of brooding after the deaths of his wife and mother. Both men needed desperately to believe that there would be a continuing line of Rutledge leadership guiding the destiny of South Carolina. Henry could not bring himself to disappoint either his father or his uncle. He patiently worked with Edward and indeed made the governor's final days happy ones. Little did Henry know that both Edward and "Dictator John" would die in the year 1800, thus freeing him to leave politics and engage in business and agriculture.

Henry and Septima were married on her sixteenth birthday. The *South Carolina Gazette,* Friday, October 18, 1799, recorded:

> Married on Tuesday evening last at Sullivan's Island, by the Rev. Mr. Frost, Henry Middleton Rutledge Esq., Major in the Army of the United States, to Miss Septima Sexta Middleton, daughter of the late Arthur Middleton, Esq.

Septima was radiant in her white satin Empire dress. It had short puffed sleeves and a low neckline. Its high waist accented her young figure giving her the appearance of royalty. Her long chemise of the finest white flannel, and her white silk stockings were each exquisitely embroidered. Her auburn locks shone through a short Brussels lace veil. She wore a pair of green sharkskin slippers.

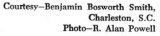

Rutledge Coat of Arms   **Middleton Coat of Arms**

The ceremony followed the 1789 Book of Common Prayer of the Anglican church. The wedding itself was small as Reverend Frost had advised. It would have been unwise to consider including guests from the mainland during one of the most destructive fever seasons Charleston had yet endured.

This particular epidemic was referred to as "strangers fever" because, for the most part, only new-comers to Charleston fell victim. It was feared that the following summer even the natives might not escape the violent attack. It would be the middle of November before the danger of infection would be past. This fever was unlike the disease which threatened the low-country plantations. No one dared to stay in the country past May tenth nor venture to return for any reason until after the first frost (usually around November fifteenth). It was desirable to be in Charleston during this season and most necessary in order to escape the fever. Now there was the fear of "strangers fever" in Charleston.

There had been a time when Middleton Place, on the Ashley River, was considered safe enough refuge. There was no great problem with this malarial type fever or with yellow fever until the years of occupation by the British beginning in 1781. It was then that the surge of fever reached epidemic proportions on the plantations.

Within a few years the Middletons began their annual migration to Charleston or Sullivan's Island for refuge from the fever. This wedding was a welcome occasion—quite a departure from the worries of the day. To be invited was considered an honor.

There was a great iced cake, according to family tradition, which was beautiful to behold. As was the custom, there were engraved white satin-covered boxes for the guests. These were used to carry home slices of cake for the young children.

News accounts and parish records establish the events of the week. It is interesting to read the words of Rosetta Margaret Izard, a nine-year-old cousin of Septima, to yet another cousin, Henrietta Drayton:

> Dear Henrietta
>
> Septima Middleton was married thuesday to the Honorable M^r He^{n}ry Rutledge: the same evening Arther Harry and Oliver were Christened. None of us were asked but they sent us two pieces of ice cake
>
> Adieu Dear
> Henrietta
> R M I

Miss Draton
Draton Hall

The entire week was one of excitement and pageantry. Septima's older brother Henry and his wife Mary Helen had returned from their extensive travels in Europe with their three sons. They took the opportunity of such a massive family gathering to have their three sons baptized. The service was on Sunday afternoon, October 13, 1799, probably followed by dinner and a reception.

Henry (heir to Middleton Place) and Mary Helen Hering had been married in 1794 in Bath, England, at the Hering family home Heybridge Hall. They had not been in Charleston long enough to receive visitors, and many family members had never met Mary Helen. Henry and Mary Helen's fashionable Sullivan's Island home was a beautiful setting for the week's festivities.

Septima had corresponded with her sister-in-law, and it made her happy to have these three precious nephews baptized the same week as her wedding. Septima knew it was meaningful to Henry to have Henry Middleton and his wife and children arrive in America. They had been a close contact for him while he was in London and Paris. They had enjoyed the opera and many social events together. Henry Rutledge had formed an attachment to Septima's nephews, Arthur and Henry; although when he left France, Arthur was three and little Henry, or Harry as they called him, was only one. Oliver Hering had been born just the year before, and all the family was happy to have the proprietor of Middleton Place and his family in their midst at last.

Three baptisms and a wedding for the Middleton family all in one week—it was almost as if Septima and Henry were beginning their married years as part of a great celebration of life.

By the close of November, 1799, Septima and Henry were settled in their fine home on Front Street at Federal Green in Charleston. Henry had been honorably discharged as Major of the 5th Infantry, U. S. Army, on July 12, 1799, just three months prior to his marriage to Septima. He had immediately begun his duties as an aide to his father partly due to the Governor's failing health and partly in preparation for entering the legislature himself.

For Septima, much of her training and education was now invaluable as she became mistress of her own home. In fact, some ninety-nine servants had been given to her as part of her extensive dowry, though a great number remained at Middleton Place until she and Henry could build a plantation of their own. Young Mr. and Mrs. Henry Middleton Rutledge were soon happily engaged in preparations for the coming holiday season.

Septima busied herself with making an inventory of the wedding silver and linen, which included a fine blue damask cloth and large dinner napkins with embroidered stars and moons, a gift to her mother and father at the Signing of the Declaration of Independence in 1776.

Governor Rutledge wanted help with his entertaining at Christmas, and there were many other events ahead for the new bride, including her sister Louisa's marriage to Daniel Blake on January 1.

The 1799 Christmas season was a happy one for Septima. Even though a newlywed, she quickly assumed her social position as wife of the governor's son. Her home was readied for the festivities just as she had planned. The competent young bride dazzled Charleston's elite with her quiet charm, engaging wit, manners, and musical ability.

One account relates the splendid dance and evening of entertainment given by Mr. Frost early in December of 1799. For now, thoughts of the dreaded fever were put aside, and energy was reserved for gala celebrations.

The party given by Mr. Frost was by invitation only and featured a numerous assemblage of the first families, among whom were Governor and Mrs. Rutledge. Septima and Henry were a popular addition to any guest list, as were Mary Middleton, her daughters Louisa and Bell, and their fiancés, Daniel Blake and Congressman Daniel Huger, respectively.

In January, 1800, Edward Rutledge traveled to Columbia for the legislature during a time when the weather was unusually bad. The *City Gazette* reported a snowfall of from six to seven inches in Charleston, which started on Thursday January 9, and lasted until midnight Friday.

Governor Rutledge was in failing health, and his return to Charleston in such inclement weather caused a rapid decline in his strength resulting in a fatal stroke. The governor's untimely death at fifty on January 23, 1800, nearly a year before his term had expired, was a shock, not only to his family, but a cause of grief for the entire state of South Carolina. The *City Gazette,* January 25, 1800, carried the following death notice:

> We announce to the public with infinite concern, the decease of our valuable fellow Citizen, His Excellency Edward Rutledge Esq. Governor and Commander in Chief of this State, who closed on Thursday night a life of fifty years devoted to the cause of philanthropy and the interests of his country . . . .

Edward Rutledge was buried in St. Philip's churchyard in Charleston.

On July 18, he was followed in death by his brother John. The *City Gazette,* July 24, 1800, contained an eloquently worded notice commemorating the life and passing of the state's first governor.

> Died, the honorable *John Rutledge* Esq. This gentleman was a Member of the first Congress in 1765, in which Situation though very young he displayed talents that excited universal admiration. In the year 1774, when South Carolina delegated unlimited powers to five of her citizens to meet in Congress with other delegates from British Provinces, to take care of their common interest, he was elected one of the five.
>
> In the year 1776, when the People of this State adopted their first independent Constitution, he was called forth to the exercise of the supreme executive authority. In the year 1779, when the State was about to be invaded, he was again invested with the same high office, with a further delegation resembling that of the Roman Dictators. These ample powers he possessed and exercised for the good of the State, for three years, and 'til civil Government was re-established in the year 1782. In the times that tried men's souls, and when the greatest abilities were requisite, Carolina looked to her John Rutledge, and confided her most important interests to his Talents and Virtues. Nor was She disappointed. What could be done by any man for his Country, invaded, distressed and overrun, was done for South Carolina by this her highly favored Son. As a Public Speaker, he charmed and transported all who heard him: his eloquence would not suffer by a comparison with the most famous orators of antiquity. He possessed an irresistable manner of address, which forced its way to the heart, and controlled every power of the Soul.

These two brothers, though ten years apart in age, had lost their wives and their mother the same year (1792), and then eight years later, died within six months of each other. Together with the early death of Arthur Middleton and the passing of other proud members of the Rutledge and Middleton families who had fought for American freedom, the deaths of John and Edward signaled the close of a dramatic era in South Carolina's history. Septima and Henry had a grave responsibility to preserve as much of their heritage as possible for future generations.

Chapter Four

Septima and Henry celebrated their first wedding anniversary, October 15, 1800. Septima had just learned that she was expecting their first child the following June. She and Henry must have been delighted with that news. There had been enough sadness their first year of marriage. Now there were happy thoughts of the new baby and of Septima's sister Bell's forthcoming marriage on November 26 to Senator Daniel Huger.

Henry knew the Revolution was costly and was not surprised that there had been little for Edward Rutledge to leave to his children, Henry and Sally, nor even to his second wife, Mary.

Of utmost importance to Henry were the Revolutionary War grants which his father Edward had purchased for five thousand pounds from John Rutledge in January, 1797. On carefully assessing their value, Henry was surprised to learn that they included 73,000 acres in the new state of Tennessee.

Ironically, Edward Rutledge had pushed for passage of the Primogeniture Act, meaning that now, Henry, as his eldest son, would not automatically inherit this land. Henry, therefore, made arrangements to sell the property to his best friend, Thomas Shubrick, for 535 English pounds: then Henry bought back his own father's property for the same nominal amount, thus guaranteeing his ownership.

Henry actually made the first journey to inspect his property in 1807. There was still unrest with the Indians, and the lands to the west must have seemed quite foreign to young Rutledge.

Henry's good friend from his days at Columbia University, John Randolph of Roanoke, often wrote to Henry, urging him to contact Andrew Jackson about his landholdings and to be careful to follow Jackson's advice. Henry heeded his friend's advice, knowing that he was well acquainted with Jackson. John Randolph was probably correct in his assessment of the situation. Henry's friend Randolph had always wanted what was best for him and Henry could trust what he said, for Randolph knew Andrew Jackson to be in touch with the particulars of land values and that he would most assuredly be one of the finest contacts in the matter of the Tennessee property.

Henry knew that his father believed there could be security for them in that land, and somehow this would be something to fulfill those expectations. Henry enjoyed the law and the way he could be of service to those who could not speak well for themselves. Even with that satisfaction and the work ahead with the legislature, he remained troubled by his own lack of ambition in seeking public office. He felt the need to reach out toward a future in another place and envisioned the challenge of helping to settle a new state. It was a desperate need of his to become more than his father's shadow.

Septima understood that they both must be concerned with an awesome heritage. Their fathers had risked everything for their country. Part of what they would have had them do is be willing to take risks. She reminded Henry that his father wanted him to be well prepared in his profession and to be part of the development of their infant nation. They were overwhelmed at times by the responsibility they had inherited.

Henry was now twenty-five, and he and Septima were celebrating not only their first wedding anniversary but also her seventeenth birthday. Henry admired the maturity Septima demonstrated in

Courtesy—Tennessee Historical Society

**John Randolph
of Roanoke
(1773-1833)**

managing their home and social obligations. He enjoyed sharing his thoughts about the future with her, knowing that she cared about his feelings.

Henry's father had advised him before the mission to France, " 'avail yourself of your situation.' " With the possibility of developing the land which now belonged to him, Henry continued to ponder the possibility of a move to Tennessee, the risk involved, and the vast possibilities such a venture offered.

Chapter Five

The years that followed were happy ones for Septima and Henry. Their first child, a girl, was born June 18, 1801, and was named Mary Middleton Rutledge for her maternal grandmother. The birth of Mary Middleton Rutledge was followed by the births of two sons, Edward Augustus Rutledge in 1802 and Henry Adolphus Rutledge on August 8, 1805.

During these years Henry managed to complete the business his father had left unfinished at his death. Septima was proud of him. She knew there were many demands on his time and yet he was always attentive to the needs of his family.

One thing in particular fascinated Septima about Henry. He was often asked to speak to various groups and accepted these invitations readily enough. He was an eloquent and forceful speaker and yet he insisted to her privately that these occasions made him very uncomfortable and nervous. She learned more with each passing year that her husband thought himself ill-suited for public life.

Henry was a member of the American Revolution Society and seemed to be their choice as orator for patriotic events. He could draw on not only his family background but also his expertise in foreign matters.

One memorable Fourth of July in 1804, Henry delivered an oration in St. Philip's Church at the request of the American Revolution Society and also of the South Carolina State Society of the Cincinnati. How proud Septima must have been as she listened to his words and thought about Arthur Middleton, Edward Rutledge, and all the others who had struggled for American independence.

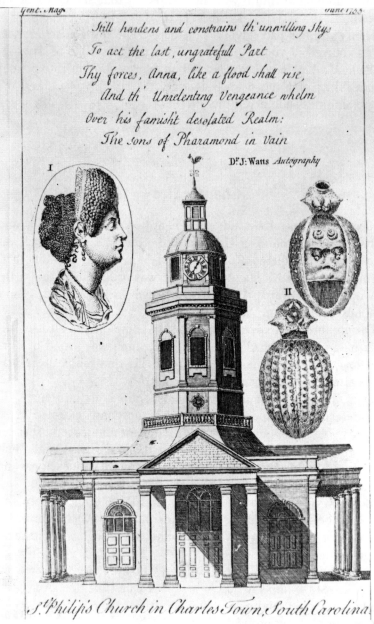

from *Gentleman's Magazine* (London) 1755
Courtesy—South Carolina Historical Society

St. Phillip's Church (1723-1835)

The exuberant crowd listened in hushed silence as the son of their late governor spoke of the impact of the Revolution on their lives:

> . . . If the revolution reflects immortal honor on those who were instrumental in achieving it, how incumbent it is on those, who succeed them in the councils of the nation, and who could not participate in the glory, at least to preserve the advantages of it. . . . With the accession of strength, which we have already gained, what have we to fear from the enmity of foreign powers, if we remain but true to ourselves: provided we are careful to keep alive, those sparks which blazed forth, and which shed so bright a gleam over the American character, during the war of the revolution? In all questions, which involve the national character, let the voice of the party be hushed—let us evince a constant unanimity in maintaining the dignity and independence of the American people. Then, indeed, shall we command the respect of surrounding nations—Then, indeed, may it with justice be pronounced, that we are still worthy of the blood which has been shed in the cause of liberty.

How the shouts and cheers must have greeted this one who quietly and with great dignity stirred the hearts of all Charleston. Henry Middleton Rutledge remembered and revered the efforts of the past which gave his generation a free land to preserve and enjoy. He and Septima never wavered in their dedication to the principles of freedom which they had inherited.

The Rutledge family seemed well established in 1807 when Henry was required to travel to Tennessee to inspect and survey his property there.

By this time, Septima's mother had given Henry part of her vast holdings across the Ashley River from Middleton Place. Henry had built a large two story frame house on a high brick foundation on the plantation he and Septima called Janesse. This home for the growing Rutledge family was on 924 acres and was comprised of parts of the Jenys and Canteys tracts which adjoined Mrs. Middleton's own Izard homeplace, Cedar Grove. There was now ample space for all of Septima's slaves as well as for those owned by Henry. The out-buildings included a row of slave cabins for their

Rumblings, reasons, for possible move. —

"people." Little is known about their years at Janesse other than the births of their children and the general social activities of Charleston and the low-country plantations.

These must have been restless years for Henry Rutledge. His cousin, Sally, and stepmother, Mary Rutledge, spent much of their time in Europe. Thomas Pinckney, Jr. in correspondence to his cousin, Harriott, at Hampton plantation, mentioned frequently their presence at the theatre in Charleston, as well as at weekend outings and picnics the young people called maroons. This was prior to 1805.

Septima's mother became more and more domineering as each of her children married. She had always spent part of each year at Cedar Grove on the Ashley River. Now with her oldest son Henry and his wife Mary Helen completely in charge of Middleton Place, she tried to assure her daughters and young, son, John Izard, of proper estates near her.

It must have been particularly hard for Septima's husband to continually accept Middleton help. He evidently needed to fulfill his desire to manage property of his own. There was much conflict over these matters, as some family letters indicate. Most likely Henry would not continue in a position of public service just because his family expected it of him. He also would make every effort to refrain from accepting any Middleton assistance.

In the years between 1801 and 1810, Septima's brother Henry was successively a representative, a senator, and finally governor of the state of South Carolina.

Henry Rutledge did serve two terms in the legislature during that time, but did not aspire to higher public office. Consequently he found more and more opportunities to develop his land in Tennessee. Of ultimate concern to Septima and Henry was the possibility of a move to Franklin County, Tennessee, and their Elk River valley land.

Septima was apparently a strong and determined woman, ever anxious to insure her husband's happiness. Their ties in Charleston were extremely secure, and yet Septima knew full well that great ventures would always involve risk if they were to be of any worth.

She encouraged Henry to make his journey and not only prayed for his safety, but for peace to come in whatever decision he would make. She searched the depths of her being for acceptance of an eventual exile from family and friends. She trusted her beloved Henry and anxiously awaited some good word from him.

Septima and Henry were very close to her sister Emma and Emma's husband, Henry Izard. The two men were both interested in their landholdings in other states and often shared their dreams of developing their property. It was only natural for Henry's correspondence with his brother-in-law to include a detailed description of his travels to Tennessee, the places he stayed along the way, and the political concerns he discovered to the west of the Carolinas.

By the middle of March, 1807, Henry had arrived in Nashville, Tennessee, following a most despicable journey. For seven days in the month preceeding Henry's arrival, the weather in Nashville and surrounding areas had stayed at a minus 5 degrees, leaving an unusual amount of ice and snow in the higher elevations. Upon passing the Blue Ridge he had experienced so much snow and mud that he commented to Izard (as he called his brother-in-law), "I would very willingly, for my own accomodations have given all the good soil I saw, for a narrow strip of our sand."

Henry, nevertheless, made his way to the home of William P. Anderson, a well-known surveyor and a friend of Andrew Jackson. Jackson was at that time involved in the development of 320 acres of land on the Stones River, known as the Clover Bottom Turf. Anderson's business dealings with Jackson concerned their mutual interest in horses.

There was a general store, boatyard, racetrack, tavern and house of entertainment on this site just seven miles from Nashville and four miles from Jackson's home. Dry goods for the store were bought in Philadelphia and then traded rather than sold. The local goods were then shipped by flatboat down the Cumberland, Ohio, and Mississippi rivers to be sold for whatever price they could bring in Natchez and New Orleans.

Henry and Jackson must have enjoyed exchanging tales about their mutual friend John Randolph when they visited the popular racetrack at Clover Bottom. Jackson's horse, Truxton, was a great attraction in the match races and sweepstakes. In fact, an argument over payment of a race forfeit eventually led to the duel, in May 1806, in which Jackson killed Charles Dickinson.

It was there at Clover Bottom that Henry met Jackson's partners, John Hutchings and John Coffee. These men would later be valuable contacts for Henry Rutledge in land speculation and business ventures in Tennessee.

Henry and William Anderson spent some few days with General Jackson before traveling on to Nashville. The conversation there included inquiries from Jackson concerning Henry Izard and others of his acquaintance in Charleston. They discussed Henry's land grants and the best approach to take in assessing their value.

They talked in depth on the most common topic of the day, namely, Colonel Aaron Burr. Henry commented on this in a letter to his brother-in-law, Izard. "I have not seen a single person who believes that Burr ever intended to attempt a separation of the Western from the Atlantic states, or to possess himself of N. Orleans."

Henry remained another ten days in Nashville at a hostelry which had been established in 1796 by Major William T. Lewis. It became Winn's Inn in 1806 and later was known simply as the Nashville Inn.

In reference to the inspection of his property, Henry wrote Izard:

> I shall set out in ten days for Elk River, where I suppose I shall be under the necessity of passing a week or two 'a la bivouac.' Anderson is now there superintending the running of his Sectional lines. I have on my hands, the agreeable task of *settling* a dispute between him & a Surveyor of the name of Hickman, on the compromising of which, depends my finding the situation of 50,000 acres of land —on the whole I think it fortunate that I prevailed on myself to take this unpleasant ride.

Henry informed Izard not to take the trouble of writing as he would have no way of receiving mail. The area between the Duck and Elk rivers was still wilderness, and travel there would be restricted to the ridges, the Indian and buffalo paths, and the creek bottoms.

Despite the discomfort of this initial journey, Henry was much taken with the natural beauty of his landholdings. He also arranged to return, with a number of his slaves from Janesse, in order to clear part of his land for farming and for the construction of a log dwelling.

Henry must have been anxious to share what he saw and learned with Septima. It is probable to imagine that his correspondence was more reassuring once he had completed the survey in Tennessee. Somehow he had to portray the awesome splendor of the Elk River, the pleasant green valley, and the surrounding Cumberland Plateau in the most appealing manner when he reached Janesse and talked with Septima.

Septima thought of the lands to the west as still uncivilized and must have wondered what disposition Henry would make of the 73,000 acres in Tennessee his father had bought from uncle John Rutledge. These Revolutionary War grants were originally land belonging to the state of North Carolina, but now had become part of the state of Tennessee. In 1806 a Tennessee Land Act made it necessary for Henry to inspect his holdings and secure his claim. He had stayed in close contact with Thomas Shubrick as to the legalities involved, and as usual Henry handled these business matters with the utmost propriety. His law practice was important, but Henry needed the security only this land in Tennessee could afford him. The adjustment would not be easy, and he was sure it would be several years before he and Septima would settle in Tennessee.

Chapter Six

Septima's fourth child was born in 1807 before Henry's return to Tennessee. They named her Henrietta Middleton Rutledge for her paternal grandmother, and she was a delight to the other children as well as to her parents.

For the next few years Henry journeyed annually to Tennessee, more assured than ever that he wanted to make this his permanent home. He contracted with Anderson and Strother, the surveyors who had been of such great assistance to him, to begin construction of a plantation house. It was to be located on the Elk River (the Indians called it Chuwallee or "singing river"). A 30x30 log house was erected first for the workers and also for Henry on his visits there. He and Septima chose an Indian name for their plantation. It was to be called Chilhowee, which meant "place of the running deer."

For Septima, it became harder and harder to imagine her husband's animation over this foreign spot, yet she found herself longing to go there and see the wild beauty he described.

Much had transpired since the death of Edward Rutledge. His second wife, Mary, and daughter Sally, traveled to Europe where they extended their stay. Mary Rutledge wrote Henry in August of 1808 encouraging him to keep his lands in Tennessee. She longed to see Henry's children and told him how she and Sally loved their letters from Septima.

My dear son,

We were made happy yesterday by a letter from our dear Septima to Sally, given us such a particular & pleasing account of yourselves, & my little darling grand-children—that I would give a great deal, if I would have been transported for a time into your memory— our sweet little Mary's perfections have reach'd us from quarters— less interested, in their descriptions, but not less pleasing—than those we have from time to time received from the dear & happy Parents; —long may these blessings continue to crown your days with joy, & your nights with peace,—I often regret that I am the means of depriving my amiable affectionate Sarah of so much delight as she would find in those near dear & interesting little Relatives; —but the pleasures she sacrifices to me now—will I hope hereafter be amply made up to her;—her society is a great comfort to me— from the love & friendship we bear each other—I believe mine is equally so to her—while I live—there is not much chance of our separating— . . . I should have written you, by the first opportunity —but waited in hopes of hearing from my Brother—as you told me —you had had some conversation with him respecting the Tennessee lands—& he promised to write me fully on the subject—I believe he has, but I have not received his letter— . . . I suppose at the time you receive this you will have returned from your Western journey —I hope it proved less irksome & unpleasant than the last—I still hold my opinion of not selling just now— . . . a few years hence it will greatly encrease in value.—Pray remember me affectionately to Mrs. Middleton and Mrs. Izard—my kindest love to Septima—Kiss the sweet little group for me— . . . Accept yourself my dear Henry the best good wishes of Yr truly & sincerely affectionate Mother

M.R.—

Septima's younger brother, John Izard Middleton, traveled to Italy and France following his mother's death. The fortune he inherited from Mary Middleton allowed him to remain in Europe where he became well known as a naturalist, archeologist, and artist. There he met Eliza Falconet, and they were married on June 11, 1810. Two years after his marriage, he published in London a volume with numerous colored plates, a collection of his own very accurate drawings: *Grecian Remains in Italy, a description of Cyclopian Walls and of Roman Antiquities with Topographical and Picturesque Views of Ancient Latium.*

It was during this period that Septima's older brother Henry was serving as governor of South Carolina. Their sisters Bell, Louisa, and Emma were all settled with families of their own.

Arthur Middleton's widow, Mary, was aging and had chosen to spend most of her time with Septima. She had given her birthplace, Cedar Grove, to John Izard and Eliza in hopes they would come to America. Mary Izard Middleton wanted her children and grandchildren near her and demanded their devotion and attention.

On February 15, 1812, Charles Cotesworth Pinckney wrote to Henry from Santee about business matters. He considered Henry more than a nephew and endeavored to encourage him whenever possible. The crops at Henry's plantation, Janesse, had been very poor, the price of cotton was extremely low, and Henry's Uncle Pinckney assured him that he would continue to cover his losses until he could make a good crop which would sell at a reasonable price.

Their friendship was longstanding and included their families. The letter closed, "your affectionate Uncle, Charles Cotesworth Pinckney," with a note of invitation following:

> My Daughters write with me in love to Septima, you and your Children; & we all hope we shall see you both, & as many of the Children as you can bring with you, in the spring at the Island—we shall be there the end of this month.

Middleton, Rutledge, Pinckney—families interwoven for generations in the strong fabric of American destiny. The parental struggle had been so costly—the birth so painful—the promotion of America's existence was completely bound by the relationships of these sons and daughters, children all of independence.

It is not hard to envision a gathering of these families at Pinckney Island near Charleston. Henry Rutledge would have much exciting news from his latest annual visit to Tennessee. He would talk to his uncle Pinckney, Septima, and indeed any who would listen about the progress on the plantation house at Chilhowee in Franklin County, Tennessee.

The original 30x30 log structure had served as quarters for the workmen as they cleared an adjoining site for an identical two story 30x30 log house. The two buildings were connected by a ten-foot covered dog trot.

Clay from the property had been hand-pressed and fired for the brick fireplaces and chimneys. Just that year the entire house had been weather-boarded and painted. The area natives called it a painted mansion.

Window casings, mantels, and doors were made from the timber of the trees that were cut to clear the hill. Between the house and the ford over the Elk River was a cave with a natural spring. Very soon Henry planned to add silk curtains to the walnut and oak framed windows, fine Brussels carpets to the yellow pine floors, and other touches of color and elegance, both native and imported; then hopefully at some point in the future, Septima and the children would add the warmth and charm needed to grace the Tennessee wilderness.

His descriptions captivated the imaginations of even the youngest of his children, and they shared their father's stories with their Pinckney cousins. They loved to tell about the piglet who wandered too close to the brickyard leaving his hoof prints in the fresh clay. Years later they would point out the unique markings to their own children.

In that same year of 1812, Septima had a fifth child, Emma Middleton Rutledge. The following year, Septima's sister Emma Izard, the baby's godmother, died, leaving her husband, Henry Izard, much distraught. It had been a long illness, and Septima and her mother rarely had left Emma's bedside.

Henry Izard remarried before a full year's mourning period was over; Henry Rutledge stayed longer than ever in Tennessee, overseeing his plantation; Henry Middleton, referred to quite often as "icy-hearted" by his relatives, attended to political concerns far more than to his sister's illness or his mother's emotional needs. Not one male family member was supportive during this long period of stress, a fact which contributed, some believe, to Mary Middleton's death.

**Miniature of
Mary Izard Middleton
(1747-1814)
artist unknown**

The matriarch of Middleton Place and Cedar Grove was at her daughter Septima's Charleston home in July of 1814 when, with no warning, she suffered a stroke. She was left without speech, completely paralyzed on her right side, and died within three weeks.

In the midst of this sadness, Septima, and indeed the entire family, was extremely thankful for Henry's safe return to South Carolina. A permanent removal to Tennessee became more feasible following the death of Septima's mother. The events of the spring of 1815 hastened their ultimate decision.

Septima's brother, John Izard Middleton, and his wife, Eliza, lost two infants while they were living in Europe. In an attempt to relieve Eliza from her depression, the couple moved to South Carolina and Cedar Grove plantation as Mary Middleton had hoped they would.

Septima was glad to have her brother so near. She became very attached to their remaining child, a daughter Anna, who was two years old. She and Septima's little Emma loved playing together.

The first of May that year signaled the beginning of the fever season and thus the return to Charleston of the low-country families. However, Septima's brother and sister-in-law stayed one day too long at Cedar Grove, and two-year-old Anna contracted the fever and died. Septima's niece was buried immediately. John and Eliza Middleton soon made plans to return to Europe.

Septima and Henry made their decision to leave the following year for Tennessee and their land near the Cumberland Mountains. Their painted mansion on the Elk River would be a welcome exile from political and social pressures as well as from the ever present fever epidemics. Chilhowee was already providing a profitable income, which could only increase with Henry there to manage his own affairs. The spring of 1816 would herald the beginning of a new life for Septima. At thirty-two she would become one of a new breed of pioneers, a striking example of culture and dignity in the midst of the Tennessee wilderness.

Part IV

CHILHOWEE

(1816-1820)

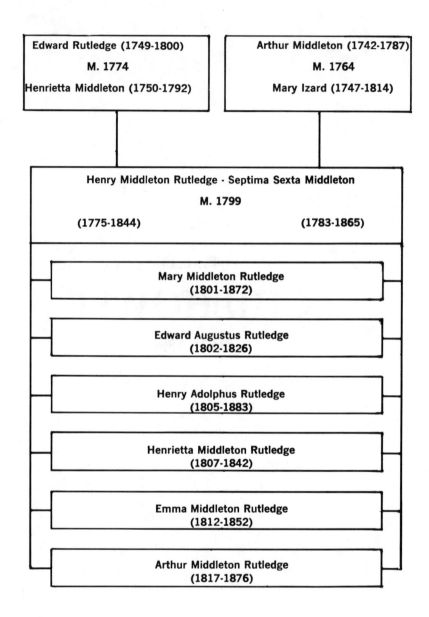

Genealogy IV—Chilhowee (1816-1820)

Chapter Seven

Following months of preparation, Septima and Henry Rutledge departed Charleston, South Carolina, for their plantation in Franklin County, Tennessee. The year was 1816. Septima was thirty-two; Henry was forty. Their five children ranged in age from four to fifteen. It was a daring venture for ones so accustomed to refinement and culture.

Passage through the Carolina mountain ranges across the Blue Ridge was not practical for a wagon train. Consequently, Henry carefully planned to travel through South Carolina to Augusta, Georgia, then along the Federal Road past Joseph Vann's home at Spring Place, where they probably spent several days resting. Joseph's father James had died in 1809.

He had sponsored the Moravian Mission school, in 1801, and was quite influential with the Cherokee people. James' mother was Cherokee, but his father, Clement Vann, was a prominent Scottish trader, and his son "Rich Joe Vann" remained much in control of affairs there. The Rutledge clan was probably quite relieved to get this far along, and the sighting of Vann's home must have cheered them. Although the Federal Road was completed, there was much room for improvement between Augusta and Spring Place.

The bricks for this two-story home were made of their own Georgia clay. The handwrought nails and hinges were made right there in James Vann's own blacksmith shop.

There were arched and columned overmantels surmounted by formal cornices, but the decorations of blue, red, green, and yellow, which prevailed all over the house, reflected North Georgia's nature itself—blue sky, red clay, green trees, and yellow-ripened grain.

The surrounding countryside was indeed interesting, being planted mostly in peach and apple trees—nothing formal in the way of gardens, yet a plantation worthy of note in this otherwise wilderness area.

The lumbering, westward-moving procession of twenty covered wagons, over fifty slaves, and a variety of livestock must have been a curious sight. It was obvious that this noble man on horseback was leading his entire family, along with all their possessions, toward a permanent settlement.

Five of the wagons were filled with furniture, two with trunks of clothes, five well stocked with food and provisions. This left seven wagons to carry a huge library of books, farm tools and implements, plus a single cart that carefully transported Septima's fine golden Italian harp.

There was an elegant carriage and four which held Septima and the girls. Mary was fifteen and able to help with nine-year-old Henrietta and little Emma who was only three. The boys rode ahead on horseback. Edward Augustus was fourteen, Henry Adolphus eleven, and they were both a great help to their father as they watched for mud holes along the circuitous route. In the fall they were to attend St. Mary's Roman Catholic school in Baltimore, Maryland. Their lives were much involved with change. Indeed all of the children were the envy of their Charleston cousins because of this venture westward.

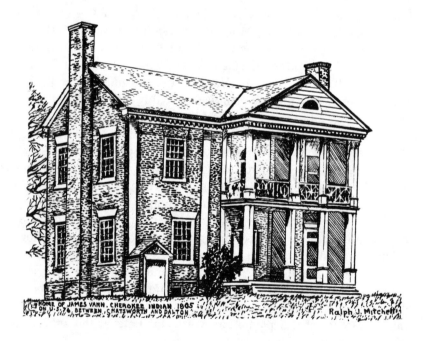

Courtesy—The Parks and Historic Sites Division of the Georgia Department of Natural Resources

Vann House, Spring Place, Georgia. This two-story brick showplace of the Cherokee Nation combines Federal architecture with the American Georgian style.

Immigration into Middle Tennessee or the "Mero District" had been heavy since April 1807. At that time the *Knoxville Gazette* reported that new people were coming into the state at the rate of two hundred a day. By 1810 the free white population had increased 137 percent, and the number of slaves had increased 238 percent.

These early settlers were stern and independent and much dedicated to simplicity. By 1814 a courthouse had been erected in Winchester in Franklin County. The rough road over the Cumberland Plateau had at times been crowded with the wagons and carts of these new settlers. Now in 1816 the vast area belonging to Henry Rutledge had been developed with care in anticipation of the arrival of his household.

Travel at best was unpleasant, and there must have been more than a few anxious moments as the Rutledge cavalcade moved into Tennessee, closer and closer to its final destination, Chilhowee.

They continued traveling northwest through Georgia from Spring Place. The wagons passed through Ross's Gap and came to a spot on Chattanooga Creek where Daniel Ross had a store and kept a stand for travelers.

There was a good frame house belonging to Ross, a cluster of log houses, and also stables and stake-and-rider fence lots. The Cherokee and mixed-blood Scots were enterprising in their provision of accommodations for the traveling public.

The wagon train would take advantage of this rest stop to make necessary repairs. Septima, Henry, and the children were probably quite ready for a hot meal and the wide cheery fireplace of the tavern's main room.

The counties in Tennessee had established fixed rates to be charged at these taverns. This was not a problem for Henry Rutledge, but some complained that two shillings for dinner and a shilling sixpence for breakfast and supper was outrageous. The high prices were generally blamed on the speculative tendency of the western movement. Traffic increased the closer they got to Tennessee. There was more than one large wagon drawn by four oxen. These wagons were loaded with flour and whiskey. Those two commodities must have been considered real necessities in the Tennessee backwoods.

The journey from Charleston, South Carolina, to Franklin County, Tennessee, for the Henry Rutledge family and their impressive caravan had taken six arduous weeks. There was great thanksgiving at having arrived safely, despite the many discomforts traveling by wagon train necessarily had entailed.

Chilhowee was all that Henry had promised Septima and soon became home for this branch of the Rutledge family. By the end of their first year in Franklin County it was hard to believe that there had ever been any question about their settling in Tennessee.

Situated atop the steep north bank of the Elk River, Chilhowee was surrounded by a fertile valley. Facing Roark's Cove and the Cumberland Plateau to the east and south, the picturesque two-story manor house, Septima's boarded, painted mansion quickly became a lively hub for the cotton plantation's activities. The horse stables were set in a grove of hackberry, sweet gum, and oak trees. Mountain chestnut and maple trees graced the knoll-top location of the Rutledge family dwelling.

This woodland exile combined the interior elegance of mahogany, crystal, silver, candlelight, and music—all the luxuries known to the South Carolina low-country planters—with the distinct advantages attributed to the healthier year-round climate.

Seasonal changes were certainly more pronounced: summer's heat, simmering and intense, never stifled the emerald breezes and azure days; fall's brilliance, blazing across the mountainous landscape, beckoned to be captured; winter's cold, glazing the rocks and ripples of the "singing river," frosted the valley and hills beyond, often draping the fields in white velveted splendor; spring's glory, bounding forth with bull nettles, brier blossoms, and dandelions, crowned the primeval wilderness, budding and bursting to herald the newness of the earth.

At the close of the first year's full cycle, as if to announce the coming of spring, on April 1, 1817, Septima and Henry welcomed the birth of a son, Arthur Middleton Rutledge.

The older boys, Edward and Henry, attended St. Mary's Roman Catholic school in Baltimore, Maryland. This well-known boys academy, according to Bishop John Carroll of the Baltimore diocese, excelled in discipline and the French language; and, as a matter of principle, it accepted students of every faith. The headmaster, Father Louis Dubourg, a West Indian of French descent, tolerated no nonsense and worked with the faculty and students in a stern, patient, and remarkable manner.

This attitude was agreeable to Septima, who required her children to speak French exclusively on Fridays. She was especially concerned that Mary, Henrietta, and Emma not forget the training they had received while living in Charleston. Their tutor had been a Mr. Willing of Philadelphia.

Quite often the Rutledge girls passed the long winter evenings patiently working their samplers as their mother read from the Bible or her favorite volume of Milton's *Paradise Lost.*

Septima's zeal for education and religious instruction continued at Chilhowee, not only for her own children but for the Rutledge slaves as well. Each Sunday afternoon the front parlor was filled with rythmic voices joined in the chanting of hymns and the reciting, in lingering low-country gullah, of the lessons of the catechism. Septima led the opening worship service, assisted by her daughters Mary and Henrietta. Then class was taught by Mary, who years later incorporated these experiences in her published volumes entitled *Sunday School Teaching* and *A Biblical View of Church Catechism.*

In like manner, classical music was not to be forgotten. Septima played her harp and accompanied the entire family on regular occasions in order to preserve that part of their heritage.

Septima Rutledge was a determined woman, filled with an awareness of the lessons to be learned from the beauty surrounding Chilhowee. Those beginning years as Tennesseans, those months of adjustment, those days of exploration, those hours and minutes of work and pleasure, began to weave together the Rutledge tapestry, strong in tradition, ornate in textures of love and caring, bright in vision for the future.

Chapter Eight

Prior to 1820, Henry Rutledge purchased land thirty-five times. Much of this property he resold, according to Franklin County deeds, and those dealings ranged from tracts of fifty to five thousand acres.

He continued to develop Chilhowee and his country seat, with cotton as his most important money crop. Chilhowee's rich sandy loam with its clay subsoil proved ideal for the raising of cotton once the land was cleared and brought to a proper state of tillage.

As early as 1808, Eli Whitney's invention, the cotton gin, had been brought into the county from Georgia. Gins were originally run by manpower, and in a few locations by water power; but for the most part the ingenious "Horse Gin" became the standard. By 1815 there were more than a dozen gins across Franklin County, producing more cotton for marketing than all the rest of the state.

The principle dealers marketed the cotton in New Orleans. "Cotton yards" were set at points along the Elk River where the cotton was collected and stored until a "rise" made it possible to float log rafts down the Tennessee River, and then by the Ohio to the Mississippi and on to New Orleans. The trip home was overland through the country of the Choctaw and Chickasaw Indians. It was at least a thirty day treacherous voyage down four rivers and an equally perilous return journey. Skillful navigation and careful avoidance of Indians and river pirates earned a number of the "river runners" a reputation which kept their services well in demand.

The details of Henry's land speculation as well as his success with cotton in Tennessee were of particular interest to his uncle Pinckney. Henry continued to counsel with Charles Cotesworth Pinckney, never forgetting his uncle's assistance during those early years at Janesse when cotton crops failed to bring adequate prices.

Of principle concern for Henry was the raising and milling of corn for the plantation's own use. East of the ford across Elk River, the Rutledge slaves built a grist mill. Then some two hundred yards from the river they hand dug a twelve-foot-wide mill race, which when flooded generated sufficient water power to keep the millstone in motion.

Everything needed for existence in that hitherto untamed area was now available for the Rutledge household; cotton for clothing, corn and meal for bread, a fine spring under the hill between the house and the river for fresh water. The river bottom was a favorite rooting spot for hogs. There they were able to find "penny-winkles" in abundance, which supplemented their corn diet and kept them fat. In addition to hogs there was livestock to supply meat and fresh milk. Henry Rutledge was indeed one of the wealthiest and most successful men in the county, perhaps the state.

The first census record for Franklin County was taken in 1820 and listed Henry, Septima, their six children, and sixty slaves. Henry was the largest slave owner in the county, which at that time was an accurate measure of wealth.

Henry Rutledge had entered the state of Tennessee during the peak years of land speculation and cotton growing. The conflict with Britain, in 1812, had deprived the English market of new world staples so that the end of the war brought about a rise in prices and demand for cotton. Just as suddenly, in 1819, prices fell, land-owners were debt-ridden, and panic ensued. The trading and specu-lating class suffered as did a large proportion of the agricultural community. Relief was sought by the Tennessee legislature for debtors, the central feature being the establishment in Nashville of a state bank or loan office.

It is no surprise then that this forty-five-year-old son of Edward Rutledge was anxious to establish himself in the growing town of Nashville, Tennessee. The expansion of Nashville had been phe-nomenal during the years prior to the depression of 1819, and continued despite the economic transition of the state. This frontier outpost was rapidly becoming a western commercial center whose trade was important and whose social customs and activities were more and more sophisticated, especially in the areas of educational and religious culture.

Of prime consideration for Henry and Septima Rutledge was the education of their younger children. It was only natural that they decided to purchase a small town house in Nashville from a Dr. Coleman who had just moved to Huntsville, Alabama.

It is recorded by Miss Jane Thomas in *Old Days in Nashville*, that:

> It was a one story house, with five or six rooms in a row and a latticed porch in front.

It was while living in this house that Henry, in subsequent years, purchased twenty acres from Montgomery Bell and was able to oversee the building of Rose Hill and the landscaping of its terraced gardens. The location was most desirable, the closest neighbors being associated with the University. This elite group included, among others, Dr. Girard Troost, Dr. Philip Lindsley, and his son Dr. John Berrien Lindsley.

A magnificent view of the Cumberland River and the growing city of Nashville added to the intrinsic appeal of Rose Hill for Septima. The sloping terraces and trellised rose gardens led to College Street on the west, while the east side of the lawn was landscaped to the Cumberland River in cherry trees and boxwoods. A spring fed into an ornate, deeply curved, semicircular terrace.

Upon completing the construction of Rose Hill, Septima and Henry divided their time between Nashville and their plantation Chilhowee. Until this time, Septima had attempted to maintain social contact with friends and family in Charleston by wintering both there and in Philadelphia. There was a bit of family gossip concerning the frequent comment made by Henry that he "couldn't let Septima winter in Philadelphia often for fear she would break him." The source of the story's amusement, quite naturally, was speculation as to the origin of their financial security. It was still assumed that their wealth must be Septima's inheritance; therefore how could she "break him"? However, Henry Rutledge had realized his goal of creating his own economic security apart from public office and had proven to be an enterprising, successful, much-respected citizen in his adopted state. South Carolinians, still clinging to remnants of family fortunes, found it hard to accept the prosperity of this one who had dared to break with tradition by joining the westward movement.

Part V

ROSE HILL

(1821-1844)

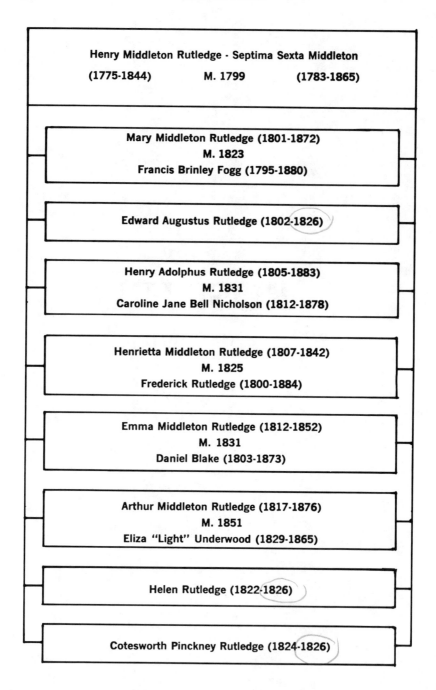

Henry Middleton Rutledge - Septima Sexta Middleton
(1775-1844)   M. 1799   (1783-1865)

Mary Middleton Rutledge (1801-1872)
M. 1823
Francis Brinley Fogg (1795-1880)

Edward Augustus Rutledge (1802-1826)

Henry Adolphus Rutledge (1805-1883)
M. 1831
Caroline Jane Bell Nicholson (1812-1878)

Henrietta Middleton Rutledge (1807-1842)
M. 1825
Frederick Rutledge (1800-1884)

Emma Middleton Rutledge (1812-1852)
M. 1831
Daniel Blake (1803-1873)

Arthur Middleton Rutledge (1817-1876)
M. 1851
Eliza "Light" Underwood (1829-1865)

Helen Rutledge (1822-1826)

Cotesworth Pinckney Rutledge (1824-1826)

Genealogy V—Rose Hill (1821-1844)

Chapter Nine

Several significant developments, in the 1820s, caused Septima and Henry to focus the family's activities around Rose Hill and Nashville. The town itself was becoming somewhat more sophisticated. In 1810, Nashville's population was eleven hundred; in 1823, thirty-five hundred. About one fourth of that number were slaves. The old public square, courthouse, and jail remained the center of the community. About it were clustered the taverns, post office, the market-house, and the principle commercial enterprises. Buildings were of brick, some even three-stories high. The majority were one- and two-story structures in Georgian style. The streets were narrow, usually unpaved, with brick or gravel sidewalks marked by curbstones. Lighting for the main streets was provided by oil lamps, and a night watch was established. Robert B. Currey was mayor, in 1822, when a stone bridge was constructed that spanned the Cumberland River just opposite the public square. The City Cemetery on South Cherry Street was open for interments.

As Septima and Henry became more involved in Nashville life, their social activities included contact with families of political prominence. This was not a result of their lineage or patriotic heritage. Their associations stemmed from their position of wealth and their cultural standing in the community as well as from their close friendship with General and Mrs. Andrew Jackson.

Rachel Jackson and Septima Rutledge shared an interest in formal gardens and helped one another make selections for landscaping of the Hermitage and Rose Hill. Andrew Jackson delighted in surprising Rachel and her friend Septima with new or rare plants and seeds he brought home from his travels. The two families visited one another and met often in connection with the most prestigous gatherings of the day. Rachel took particular interest in the Rutledge children, since she had none of her own. Her nephew Andrew Jackson Donelson became a close associate of Septima's oldest son Edward. The two young men joined General Jackson in Pensacola, Florida, in May of 1821.

Jackson had resigned from the army in order to accept the commission from President James Monroe appointing him first territorial governor in Florida. In 1819, Spain had sold all of Florida to the United States for five million dollars. Jackson then asked his wife's nephew, a lieutenant in the United States Army and recent West Point graduate, and young Edward Rutledge to serve as secretaries in the provisional government. Henry M. Brackenridge was the first alcalde or translator in 1821. He enraged Jackson by submitting a false translation of Spanish Governor Don José Callava's address during transfer negotiations. He then denied the mistake. Jackson immediately replaced Brackenridge with his trusted friend, Edward Rutledge, by the following appointment.

> Mr. Edward A. Rutledge
> Sir,
> I do hereby nominate and appoint you Translator of the Spanish Language for me, as Commissioner duly appointed under the U. States, to take possession of the Floridas, agreeably to the Treaty with Spain, concluded at the city of Washington on the 19th day of February, 1819, with all the emoluments which may be allowed by the President of the United States for the performance of said duty. Given under my hand at Montpelier this 12th day of May, 1821.
>
> (signed) Andrew Jackson,
> Commissioner
>
> Attent.—J. C. Bronaugh
> Private Secy

The conditions in Pensacola were hostile and very uncomfortable for Jackson. His wife Rachel was extremely unhappy and urged him to relinquish his position as governor and return to Tennessee. In October 1821, Jackson gave up the governorship of Florida apparently to seek an early retirement at his Tennessee home, the Hermitage. It was only a short time before three of Jackson's closest associates, William Lewis, John Eaton, and John Overton encouraged the "Hero of New Orleans" to advance his political career by running for president of the United States. As was his custom, Andrew Jackson used all the influence at his command to ensure positions for his family and friends. Lieutenant Andrew Donelson and Edward Rutledge had returned to Tennessee with Andrew and Rachel Jackson, serving for a time at the Hermitage to conclude their duties in regard to Jackson's termination as governor of Florida. Jackson arranged for Lieutenant Donelson to resume his study of law. Rutledge, however, decided to settle at Pensacola and pursue a career there. This prompted Jackson to communicate certain letters of referral to William P. Duval of Kentucky who followed as second governor of the Florida territories. It was obvious that Andrew Jackson maintained the highest regard for Edward Rutledge.

This circumstance originated, no doubt, in the early relationships, both business and social, with Edward's parents, Henry and Septima. However, Jackson apparently had been impressed with Edward's competence as translator for Florida's transitional government.

Andrew Jackson espoused a fierce loyalty toward those he counted his friends. His recommendation of nineteen-year-old Edward Rutledge showed confidence and insight into the young man's character.

Hermitage near Nashville
June 1st 1812

Dear Sir:

I have the pleasure to acknowledge the recpt of your very kind letter of the 14th ult and learning that you were preparing to proceed to Pensacola, have postponed answering until now, that it might meet you on your arrival at Pensacola. . . . Permit me barely to remark, that upon your entering on the duties assigned you, it is

—Photo by Jim Wheeler
Miniature owned by Mary Stevenson Poling and Eleanor Rutledge, Jacksonville, Ala.

Edward Augustus Rutledge (1802-1826)

only necessary to let the people know over whom you preside, that the laws will be administered with energy, and impartial Justice to all. This will give you ease, and harmony in your Territory.

I have a young friend who has gone to settle at Pensacola, he speaks, writes, and translates, the Spanish language correctly. During my administration he was my interpreter and translator of the Spanish and French languages. I can recommend him to you, as one of the most correct young gentlemen in any country. It is Mr. Edward M. Rutledge son of Major Rutledge now of Nashville formerly of Charleston. This young gentleman can say what but few others can with truth, that both of his grandfathers signed the Declaration of our Independence. Should you find it necessary to have an interpreter & translator of the French & Spanish language, in him you will find a correct one, and in him you can confide.

I see that a commission is appointed to settle the land claims in Florida. I am unacquainted with any of them but Mr. Samuel Overton—who is well acquainted with Mr. Rutledge. Can I claim your friendship in asking you to make Mr. Rutledge acquainted with Mr. Preston & Mr. Ware and to say to them he is well qualified to fill the appointment of Sec. to their board. Mr. Rutledge is modest and reclining, he will never ask for anything, but it is to be remarked, that our public offices would be generally better filled if officers, were sought for to fill offices, instead of offices being sought for, and I only bring him to your view knowing the real merit and capacity of this young gentleman and of his incorruptible morals, and as such I make him known to you, that you can benefit by his talents, and services, should you think proper to claim them. Your friend Dr. Bronaugh is well acquainted with him, and to him you can refer. . . . I would make known to you Capt Easter who with Capt Call served in my staff. . . . I have allways [sic] endeavored to have nothing but honourable and honest men around me. I have therefore named to you a few of those who I found trustworthy, with whom, any man is safe. I am sir with great respect

Yr mo, ob, servt,
Andrew Jackson

His Excellency
Wm. P. Duval
Governor of Florida

Edward Rutledge considered Andrew Jackson a valuable part of his life, much the same way his father Henry Rutledge felt toward his uncle Charles Cotesworth Pinckney. Both Jackson and Pinckney served as outstanding Generals in the United States Army, both were representatives of the government in relations with foreign powers, and both men were wise enough to develop the talents of those younger associates who could benefit from their guidance.

Edward wrote Jackson in August of 1822 to tell him of the existing conditions in Pensacola:

Pensacola, 24 Aug 1822

My dear sir,

It is now sometime since I did myself last the honor of writing you. . . . My father's last letter mentioned your design of quitting the Hermitage for a short time during the summer months to make a tour of the Springs in Kentucky for your health. This plan however I presume has not been carried into execution, as none of your letters to your friends have mentioned anything more of it. Have the goodness to present my respects very affectionately to Mrs. Jackson, who has left, I assure you an ineffacable impression in this quarter. . . . Our city, which has acquired so wide a fame for health, has this year been visited by a dry summer, which added to some local causes, and the imprudence of the American population has made it the scene of fevers of various kinds. . . . the yellow fever, which we had hoped to have never heard in this region of pure air and nature, at present resounds in every ear. . . . I am writing from a plantation near the town to which the commissioners have removed, and will endeavor before I close, to send you more exact account.

Remember me, if you please, to Lieut. Donelson. He is still I presume, at Lexington, qualifying himself for the practice of the Law. I had thought lately of following his example. . . . But have lately experienced again an . . . unaccountable distaste, which I could ascribe, after desirous and mature inspiration, to nothing but a natural disqualification for the profession, I have considered that to continue my studies would be but a waste of time and labour, and have therefore requested my Father's leave to direct my future views another way. . . . I shall probably continue to aid the Commissioner's translator until the office of the Secretary shall be vacant, which there is reason to believe will be the case some months hence, . . . Should I accompany the Commissioner to St. Augustine in the capacity of Secretary, I shall be happy to acknowledge myself indebted, my dear Sir, to your influence and solicitude and be assured that nothing will be more acceptable to me than an opportunity of accepting either there or here any comments which yourself or Mrs. Jackson may have. . . . Your friends here are tolerably well. Capt^s Easter and Call have both been indisposed, . . . Mr. Overton already makes a very honourable impression, . . . Dr. Bronaugh's political honour seems clear and understood. His medical talents have been put into intensive requisition during the prevailing disease, and his attention has been so much devoted to others that he has rather neglected himself. He has been indisposed for a day or two past but will I hope soon be well again. Judge Brackenridge is occupied in making agricultural improvements, to this he devotes most of the leisure allowed him from the duties of the Bench.—

Augst 26—I had just left room to make a little note on arriving. . . . The sickness, I am sorry to say still continues . . . I hope to be able my dear Sir, to write to you next under more favourable auspices . . . respects if you please to Mrs. J. . . .

Your ob^t humble serv^{nt}

E. A. Rutledge

The 1822 yellow fever epidemic in Pensacola, mentioned in this letter to Jackson, was responsible for so many deaths that the legislative assembly had to be moved to Tallahassee that summer. Dr. Bronaugh died on September 2. Before his death he was considered the leading contender for election as Florida's first delegate to Congress. His death was one of personal sacrifice, as he literally had worn himself down in his constant care of the sick. Jackson sent word to Edward Rutledge to bring Dr. Bronaugh's slaves and other personal belongings to the Hermitage. In November 1822, Jackson closed the doctor's personal accounts, and with the help of his trusted friend Rutledge, delivered the servants to Bronaugh's mother in Virginia. This was just one example of the services Edward Rutledge performed for Andrew Jackson.

There is a receipt on record signed by Rutledge for $240, pay for eighty days work as Jackson's translator and interpreter May 12 until August 1, 1821. He then served as translator and interpreter for William P. Duval, actually at Jackson's request, from June 20 until September 20, 1822, at $1 per day. Following Dr. Bronaugh's death Edward escorted the servants to Tennessee and evidently stayed some time at the Hermitage, most probably working in Jackson's first campaign for president.

Edward was very much like his father, Henry, in that he did not wish to seek public office, yet his values and patriotic ideals were an ever present force in his decision to follow Andrew Jackson. In this respect he resembled his grandfather. This exemplary namesake of Edward Rutledge, the signer of the Declaration of Independence from South Carolina, seemed to embrace the courage and principles he had been taught from birth. Those "certain inalienable rights" were his to claim. And with maturity he would not seek to change his nature, but to establish it in some well chosen field.

Chapter Ten

Much may be learned about Septima and her family at Chilhowee and Rose Hill during the decade of the 1820s through family correspondence. In particular there is a collection of letters which Septima received from her sister-in-law, Mary Helen Hering Middleton. Mary Helen and Henry Middleton, Septima's older brother, were in St. Petersburg, Russia, from 1820–1829. It was during those years that Henry Middleton served, at the request of President Monroe, as American ambassador to the courts of Alexander I and his successor Nicholas I, both sons of Paul I and part of the lineage of the House of Romanov.

Mary Helen's letters are colorful, dramatic, and describe in detail the post-Napoleonic Russian Court as she observed it during festivities as well as during a period of mourning for the Empress Mother.

She wrote on November 25, 1820, of their safe arrival, of leaving her two sons in England with her brother, of seeing John Izard and Eliza Middleton and of Eliza's poor health. She added:

. . . We all unite in love to you all not forgetting Miss Rutledge when you write to her.

She was referring to Henry's sister Sarah Rutledge and inquired about her often.

Some letters were six months to a year reaching their destination, and news, both good and bad, remained mysteries only to be solved by the safe arrival of a steam packet from America to the European Continents, or vice versa. It was not until August, 1821, that Mary Helen received a letter Septima had written in April. That letter was in response to the one written by Mary Helen, November 25, 1820. On August 25, 1821, Mary Helen wrote:

> . . . You seem so much pleased with Nashville that your Friends in Phila stand but a bad chance of seeing you there again. . . .
> Do you expect Miss Rutledge to pay you a visit? . . . thank Mary for her letter. . . . You do not mention yr health, I hope I may conclude it is good.

Then on October 12, 1821, Mary Helen wrote:

> . . . What a time your letter has been coming—3 months! . . . I hope you continued to improve in health & strength after your removal to the mountains which must in the summer be far preferable to a town residence.

The mountains referred to Chilhowee and the Cumberland Plateau area of the Rutledge's Elk River plantation. Mary Helen then mentioned Septima's oldest son:

> Edward will have returned to you full of interesting information of all that he has seen in his excursions to the South. I dare say Genl Jackson will wish to keep him, as his knowledge of the languages must make him extremely useful, besides his other qualities which must ensure esteem.

In April of 1822, Mary Helen began a letter on the twenty-seventh describing a milder Russian winter than usual and the details of a ball given by the Empress Mother to celebrate the birthday of her daughter. Then in the same letter three days later she added:

> 30th I had yesterday the pleasure my dear Septima to receive your letter of the 27th Jany, & am rejoiced to find that your health is so good. I hope it will not be impaired by the solution of the mystery (as you call it) & that by the time you receive this a *little* Septima may have been welcomed. You are so fond of romantic names, you ought to add Sylvia to designate her birth place. . . . How happy you must feel to have all your family round you! I fear that will never be my case again.

The mystery was indeed solved, in June 1822, by the birth of a baby girl, a seventh child as Septima had been. Her name did not include Sylvia (latin derivation for "woodland") but rather Helen in honor of her aunt in faraway Russia.

By November of 1822, Septima wrote Mary Helen that her daughter Mary had traveled to Charleston for a visit and was expected to return with Cousin Sally Rutledge for the winter in Nashville and a possible trip for all of them to Philadelphia nearer spring.

Mary Helen responded in May 1823, to news of Septima's son Edward and his safe return the fall before to Nashville and his family:

> . . . How fortunate it has proved that Ed^d had been *seasoned* by a former attack of yellow fever from falling a victim to it, at Pensacola! but how very imprudent he was to trust himself there.

Mary Helen mentioned often a concern about Septima's daughters and their possible marriages. At one point she asked about "Mary's fixing her fate in Charleston" and proceeded to guess which eligible young men might be courting her nieces.

Septima's visits to South Carolina in the early 1820s were to maintain family ties and to introduce the older Rutledge daughters, Mary and Henrietta, into Charleston society. The girls attended the fashionable Nashville Female Academy, which had been chartered in 1817. However, social opportunities were still limited in Nashville, compared to the older, more established circles such as the St. Cecelia Society in Charleston. Septima Rutledge was eager to provide every advantage for her daughters and at the same time enjoyed visiting with her sisters, friends, and of course Cousin Sally.

Sally and her stepmother, Mary Rutledge, had returned from some twelve years in Europe and were now residing on Tradd Street in Charleston. Sally had begun her lifelong contribution to the Episcopal Sunday Schools and the Church Home for orphans there in her native city. She became well-loved and respected for her charitable work. She inspired Septima and twenty-one-year-old Mary Middleton to initiate many of the same projects in Nashville. She urged them to secure the formation of an Episcopal congregation, inquiring often as to their progress. She impressed upon them the need for secular education for the poor and that this could be provided through the church school effort.

Cousin Sally Rutledge enjoyed her visits to Nashville and Chilhowee. She was happy to see her brother Henry and his entire family involved in the founding of Christ Episcopal Church. It was in the early gatherings of Episcopal families in Nashville that Mary Middleton Rutledge met a young lawyer from Connecticut named Francis Brinley Fogg.

Chapter Eleven

On Septima and Henry's twenty-fourth wedding anniversary, October 15, 1823, their oldest child Mary Middleton married Francis Brinley Fogg, a newly elected trustee of Cumberland College.

Francis Fogg, a native of Brooklyn, Connecticut, was born September 21, 1795, the son of an Episcopal clergyman, Reverend Daniel Fogg. As a young lawyer, he journeyed to Columbia, Tennessee, in February of 1818. At the suggestion of the Honorable Felix Grundy, he moved to Nashville in the fall of the same year. Francis Fogg was described as prudent, temperate, discreet, charitable. Quiet in demeanor, unobtrusive in manner, he shrank from notoriety or prominence. He distinguished himself as a lawyer of integrity in his practice with the Honorable Ephraim Foster. Later he joined his father-in-law Henry Rutledge in attaining a new respect for justice in Nashville.

It is then of little surprise that this marriage to Mary Middleton Rutledge was of great social consequence. This was evidenced, in part, by the formal regret sent to them by Andrew Jackson on behalf of himself and his wife Rachel:

Genl A. Jackson & Lady presents their respectful compliments to Major E Rutledge & Lady, informs them that the melancholy intelligence of the deaths of Mrs. J. Sister & Niece, who were buried in the same grave, prevents Mrs. J & the General the pleasure of being at the party next Wednesday evening, present us affectionately to your family, with our best wishes for the happiness of the intended son in law and your amiable daughter.

Hermitage October 13th 1823

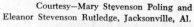

Courtesy—Mary Stevenson Poling and
Eleanor Stevenson Rutledge, Jacksonville, Al.

Photos—Jim Wheeler
Courtesy of the Tennessee Historical Society

Left—Mary Middleton Rutledge Fogg (1801-1872). Right—Francis Brinley Fogg (1795-1880), Portrait hangs in the office of the Lieutenant Governor of Tennessee.

Regarding the marriage and the family position, Mary Helen wrote Septima in February from St. Petersburg, Russia:

St Petersburg Februy 2d 1824

I received your letter of the 25th of Octr my dear Septima a few days since, announcing Mary's marriage which gave us all great pleasure, as it seems to promise great happiness—that it may long continue is my sincere wish. I cannot form a better [word missing] for your Daughter than that *her* married state may prove as blest as yours has been. Few women I think have had so much reason to be happy as you my dear Septima! I do not wonder at your agitation at the time the event took place, or the difficulty you experienced in resigning your *Treasure,* for I know the excess of your sensibility—But you say you afterwards became reconciled to a temporary separation & the meeting your friends in Charleston would no doubt tend to lessen your regret at leaving two such dear objects in Tennessee. Mary will I hope restore my little Namesake to you in perfect health & your own will I daresay have been benefitted by the journey & change of climate. I long to hear your account of your Winter in Charleston. . . .

She continues by mentioning Septima's other children:

Henrietta by your account has become quite a *Personage* & you will indulge her this winter I suppose by carrying her into public.— We were surprised to hear of Emma's presuming so soon to look over her Sister's head—We left her such a delicate little girl! Arthur was always a fine little fellow & he is I daresay as entertaining as my Friend Henry used to be at his age—You speak of *his* attending to his Profession—Has *he* then so young begun his career of the Law! It seems in truth the only profession in America in which a young man can hope to attain distinction. . . .

Life in Tennessee must have seemed very primitive to Mary Helen.

Will Miss Rutledge consent to accompany you to Tennessee? It will be a hard struggle for her between her sense of the duty she owes Mrs R. & her affection for you all, to decide. . . . You talk of traveling through the Indian nation—what a journey! I have just been looking at the map, but it is impossible for me to trace your road. I hope you found y^r way safely thro' *it*—Are your neighbors the Indians becoming civilized or do they adhere to their original customs? You will be glad to hear that my dear Children in England are all well. . . . Mr M. & the girls unite with me in offering our Congratulations and best wishes to the young Couple & love to yourself and family . . . dear Septima. Your affectionate Sister

M.H.M.

By the close of 1824 Septima had borne her eighth child, a son named Cotesworth Pinckney Rutledge in honor of Henry's uncle Charles Cotesworth Pinckney.

That same year, Andrew Jackson's unsuccessful bid for the presidency of the United States was a discouragement to all those who had supported him. Henry Rutledge received a letter from Jackson in reference to the General's campaign:

Senate Chamber
March 11th1824

Dear Major

I have this moment recd your kind & friendly letter of the 4th instant: and from the feelings of gratitude that your letter has excited in my bosom I take up my pen to acknowledge its recpt & to present you my thanks.

I cannot my Dear Sir take Carolina & Georgia on my way home, you know my feelings; my course is an old one, & I cannot at my age depart from it.

I enclose for your information the proceedings on Pennsylvania.

Present my respects to your lady & amiable family and accept for yourself a token of my friendship & Esteem

Andrew Jackson

Major H. M. Rutledge

In the national election, no electoral majority was achieved. Andrew Jackson received 99 votes, John Quincy Adams, 84, William H. Crawford, 41, and Henry Clay, 37. Thus, the election had to be decided in the House of Representatives the next year. In February of 1825, John Quincy Adams won thirteen of the twenty-four states in the Congressional election, even though Jackson had received a plurality of popular votes and of electoral votes. Jackson's supporters suspected corruption, but an official investigation was not undertaken.

John C. Calhoun of South Carolina became vice-president; Henry Clay was appointed secretary of state by Adams, and a new era emerged on the American political front. The election resulted in the split in the Democratic-Republican Party. The Adams-Clay faction became known as the National Republican Party (Whigs in the 1830s) while the pro-Jackson group retained the name of Democratic-Republican, known as the Democratic Party after 1828.

Septima and Henry Rutledge remained closely involved with Andrew and Rachel Jackson during this uncertain period. Young Edward Rutledge took the Jackson defeat poorly and resolved to work harder than ever for his much-respected hero. Mary and Francis Fogg likewise remained supportive; talk of a future victory for Jackson was common fare at private as well as social gatherings.

—Photo by Jim Wheeler
Courtesy of owners Mary Stevenson Poling
and Eleanor Stevenson Rutledge,
Jacksonville, Ala.

Courtesy—Middleton Place Foundation

Left—Septima Sexta Middleton Rutledge (1783-1865), Portrait by Edward Marchant c. 1825. Right—Henry Middleton Rutledge (1775-1844), Date of painting unknown—attributed to Cooper.

Following the election that early spring of 1825, energy was directed toward the expected reception of the Marquis de Lafayette in Nashville. It had been fifty years since this magnificent French General, at age nineteen, had played his significant role in the colonies' War of Independence.

There are many accounts of Lafayette's visit to America. Of particular significance to the Rutledge family in Tennessee was the reception in Charleston that April. On hand to greet Lafayette in Charleston were Generals Thomas and Charles Cotesworth Pinckney. These two brothers were in full regimental dress to welcome this renowned Frenchman. Charles Cotesworth was then president general of the Society of the Cincinnati and as such presented an address of welcome to their fellow member. Lafayette answered by speaking of his joy in seeing so many officers with whom he had served in America. He was well entertained while in South Carolina. Celebration was the keynote and elaborate preparations were the order of the day.

For Charles Cotesworth Pinckney it was his last public appearance. Lafayette welcomed his dear friend with a Gallic kiss on each cheek. Their conversations included many glorious reminiscences of their younger days and their beloved friend Washington. They too were bound by ties of blood as well as friendship, for by this time Lafayette's niece, Elenore Marie Florimonde de Fay la Tour Marbourg, had married the Pinckneys' nephew Daniel Horry. The Pinckneys assured Lafayette that his welcome in Tennessee would include yet another favorite nephew, Henry Middleton Rutledge.

Lafayette, his son, secretary, and entourage arrived by boat in Nashville on May 4, 1825. They disembarked at Fairfield Landing where they were received by General Andrew Jackson and the welcoming committee. Henry Rutledge was official interpreter, largely due to his time of service in France with his uncle Pinckney in 1797–1798.

Lafayette entered Nashville under an arch of flowers in a carriage drawn by four white horses. He was escorted by a large procession of citizens and soldiers. The visitors, camped around Nashville, numbered twenty thousand, although the city itself had a population at that time of only six thousand inhabitants. Lafayette stayed at the home of Dr. & Mrs. McNairy on Summer Street and was entertained lavishly by the Rutledges at Rose Hill, where he spent one night. There was a ball given in his honor at the Masonic Hall, where a supper room had been added just for the occasion. Invitations had been designed months in advance by the artist in residence at the Hermitage, Ralph E. W. Earl. Lafayette, during his time in Nashville, probably enjoyed sharing his cherished recollections of the Revolution with Septima and Henry. Middleton—Rutledge—Pinckney—names closely associated with Lafayette's warmest memories. Every effort was made to honor this one who had risked his life for the American colonies. Andrew Jackson escorted Lafayette down the river bank as he was leaving. Lafayette lingered behind being somewhat lame and the path quite steep. "Come on General," said the Hero of New Orleans who was in front. "Never mind the danger, the gods have you and me in keeping."

The remainder of 1825 brought a mixture of emotions for Henry and Septima Rutledge. On July 11, their first grandchild, a son, was born to Mary and Francis Fogg. He was named Francis

Brinley Fogg, Jr., and he immediately captivated the family's atten-
tion. On August 16, Henry's beloved uncle Charles Cotesworth
Pinckney died and was laid to rest at St. Michael's Episcopal
Church in Charleston.

Then, on October 15, their daughter Henrietta Middleton
Rutledge married her kinsman Frederick Rutledge, grandson of
old "Dictator John" Rutledge and son of Frederick and Harriott
Horry Rutledge. The ceremony was in Nashville, and Henrietta,
like her sister Mary, had chosen her parents' anniversary and
mother's birthday as her wedding date. Their home would be
Hampton Plantation on the South Santee near Charleston. Septima
expressed sorrow at the thought of being separated from her
daughter, yet found delight at Henrietta's marriage to such an
outstanding and accomplished young man.

Frederick Rutledge followed the precedent of his maternal great-
grandmother, Eliza Lucas Pinckney, in procuring the knowledge
necessary to be legal counsel, doctor, and teacher for "his people"
at Hampton and the adjoining plantations. Being a descendant of
Dr. John Rutledge of Ireland led him to study medicine at the
University of Dublin. His bride's beauty complimented his own
handsome features, and the two soon graced Charleston's most
fashionable circles.

−Courtesy of Eleanor Rutledge, Jacksonville, Alabama
Photo—Jim Wheeler

Hampton Plantation

(Obverse view)

Photo—Jim Wheeler
Courtesy—Benjamin Bosworth Smith,
Charleston, S.C.

**Frederick Rutledge (1800-1884),
artist unknown, painted c. 1825**

Private Possession
Photos—Charles N. Bayless

**Wedding Locket—
Frederick and Henrietta
Rutledge c. 1825
(Reverse view)**

Hampton Plantation, former headquarters of Francis Marion, the Revolutionary War's "Swamp Fox," had yet another distinction. In 1791, George Washington had visited there before entering Charleston while on his triumphant southern tour. Named for Hampton Court Palace in England, the plantation was laced by garden paths lined with bricks used as ballast on ships coming from England. A white-columned portico had been added to the mansion, which boasted of twenty-three sleeping rooms. The ballroom contained an immense fireplace and heart of pine floors. Each plank ran the length of the room, forty-two feet, without a seam. There was cypress paneling and a domed ceiling. Month long visits to Hampton and, of course, to Middleton Place no doubt provided many hours of pleasure for Septima and the younger children on holidays from Nashville and Chilhowee.

Chapter Twelve

The year 1826 began without ceremony for the Tennessee Rutledge family. Of significance to Rose Hill and those living near the college property, the old Cumberland College was rechartered as the University of Nashville. Septima and Henry's neighbor, the Reverend Philip Lindsley, formerly of Princeton, became its president.

The Episcopal Sunday schools were coming into being at this time, with Septima Rutledge and Mary Fogg well in the leadership. These schools were begun primarily for the secular as well as religious education of the poor and were not at first under the patronage of the church. Private support from the Rutledge and Fogg families helped establish the initial public education in Nashville. James K. Polk led the fight in the legislature for funding from the sale of lands to help establish public education in the whole state of Tennessee.

Septima was constantly aware of the needs of others. While remaining diligent in her role as a grandmother at forty-three, she was at the same time adjusting to her own "second" family—Helen was now past three years old and Cotesworth Pinckney would soon be two. Thirteen-year-old Emma was her greatest help now that Mary and Henrietta were married. Septima knew that soon she would introduce Emma to Charleston society, but for now life for them would still be divided between Chilhowee and Rose Hill.

Septima's daughter, Henrietta, and her new husband, Frederick Rutledge, joined the summer migration of southern planters and merchants to the most fashionable northern resorts. They began their summer at Saratoga Springs, New York, and ended the season at Newport, Rhode Island. The summer of 1826 was the first for them as a married couple in the resort society.

Saratoga was an attractive village of white houses with green blinds, wide streets and grand hotels. Together these hotels could accommodate eight or ten thousand people. A typical day at the Congress or the United States Hotel began early with a walk to the bubbling springs for six to twelve tumblers of the healthful water. Then there was breakfast, followed by a drive to the lake. Bowling or billiards or lounging with the necessary mint juleps or sherry cobblers were favorite ways to pass the afternoons. Dinners were served early, American style. After dinner the band would play under the trees, and there was time to saunter or lounge again while reading the New York journals. There would be a late tea, after which guests would dance the Schottische, the Waltz, or maybe the Polka. There were ice cream suppers and always enough cooling beverages to see the day through. The next day—and the next— were the same until it was time to leave for Newport, which was the nicest of the seaside resorts. The entertainment there each year would begin after the Saratoga season had ended with its "Grand Ball."

The summer of 1826 promised to be filled with the usual gaieties, and yet a tinge of sadness permeated the American scene. News quickly reached Saratoga of the deaths of former presidents Thomas Jefferson and John Adams on July 4, the fiftieth anniversary of their signing of the Declaration of Independence. It was indeed one of the most remarkable coincidences in American history. This was to be only the beginning of shock and grief for the Rutledge family.

It is known that Henrietta and Frederick Rutledge accompanied a number of low-country people from South Carolina to Saratoga that year as guests of Christopher Jenkins, of Edisto Island. Henry, Septima, and their other children were also visitors at America's most famous resort, with lodgings at the United States Hotel. Helen, who was four, and her two-year-old brother, Cotesworthy Pinckney, in some manner met with a tragic and accidental death. There is no record of a devastating fire or cholera or any other epidemic that particular summer, and yet their deaths are noted with burial in Saratoga Springs.

Evidently distraught by the deaths of his sister and brother, and weakened by a serious attack of narcolepsy (sleeping sickness), twenty-four-year-old Edward sank into irreversible depression. This fine, handsome, intelligent grandson of two signers of the Declaration of Independence, and interpreter/aid to Andrew Jackson took his own life July 16, 1826. His death is mentioned in Cornelius Durkee's *Reminiscences*:

July 16, 1826

Edward Augustus Rutledge shot himself in the United States Hotel.

A further note of explanation concerning Edward's state of health
and suicide is found in a lengthy letter from Arthur Peronneau
Hayne to Andrew Jackson:

> Ballston Springs, State of
> New York 20th July 1826

> My Dear General, Your kind letter from the Hermitage, . . . I
> received safely while in Phila in June, . . . It is with the most heart-
> felt sorrow I inform you, of the unfortunate Death, of your young
> friend, Edward Rutledge.—In a fit of *Insanity,* on Monday evening,
> he blew his brains out, with a Pistol, at the Saratoga Springs—his
> Father & family were in the house at the time. He had the Nara-
> cloid [sic] in Charleston last winter, which disease produced unusual
> debility, & depression of Spirits which notwithstanding all the
> exerting of the kindest friends continued to afflict him, & at last
> terminated in his destroying himself.—Major Rutledge is at present
> at this place with all of his family.—We know that Mrs J. & yourself
> will sympathize with the family of our lamented young friend. . . .
> believe me dear General to be your faithful & affectionate friend.
> —A. P. Hayne.

Ballston Spa was seven miles south of Saratoga and the closest rival
for the resort trade. Henry evidently moved his famly there following
Edward's suicide.

All three children of Henry and Septima were buried in Putnam
Cemetery in Saratoga Springs, New York. There lingers a mystery
concerning the three deaths—their story remains buried with them.
Septima's strength and resolute faith enabled her to recover, to
return to the agonizing details of daily existence, to provide stability
and courage for the rest of the family and solace for her husband.
Life for them would forever echo the sounds of child-like laughter;
all memories of young manhood would now be merely the elusive
reflections of light once captured by the firm, steady, gray eyes of
Edward Augustus Rutledge.

Chapter Thirteen

Following the deaths of Edward, Helen, and Cotesworth Pinckney, life at Rose Hill was not diminished by tragedy. Nashville was a booming frontier town with more legal work for Henry Rutledge than before. He was admitted to the Davidson County bar, in 1827, and spent less time overseeing his landholdings. His name was mentioned in connection with a possible appointment in Europe. There is a letter, dated May 11, 1828, to Septima from her sister-in-law, Mary Helen, written from St. Petersburg, Russia, which speaks of the comfort Septima extended her at the death of Mary Helen and Henry Middleton's daughter Eleanor. Both she and Septima lost children in the year 1826—both women sought ways to express in writing their grief as well as their sympathy for each other.

My dear Septima
    Your letter of the 20th Novr reached me about 2 months since, & this is the first opportunity I have of sending you an answer. The expression of your sympathy went to my heart—it is soothing in our affliction to know that our grief is shared by those we love. I have had full experience of the warmth of your affection & the tenderness of your heart & can always be sure of finding in your breast feelings corresponding with mine. I can readily conceive from my own state of mind, the distress you were still suffering when you wrote—Wounds such as have been inflicted on us, cannot *ever* be healed—for though we may attain an apparent tranquility, & be obliged to perform everyday duties to the rest of our families, yet the thoughts are continually recurring to the sad recollections of those whose image can never be effaced from our minds. I grieve to hear that the intensity of your feelings should have brought on the illness you mention—You say the sight of Henrietta roused you, & that you were restored to some degree of happiness. . . . you have still my dear Septima many blessings left—this I know must have been often repeated to you—it has been equally urged to me, as a reason for endeavoring to subdue my grief—but it will have its course—I sincerely hope you have now no new cause of disquiet & that all your family are enjoying health & that your own is quite reestablished. I often have thought it not improbable, if events turn

out as the newspapers had us to suppose, that Mr Rutledge may be sent to Europe as Minister either to London or Paris—Would you not like to come? . . . 15th I have had so many interruptions since this was begun that I can scarcely find time to finish it. I am anxious to hear how you have been since your last letter—better I trust both in mind & body—God bless you & sustain you my dear Septima pray y^r affectionate

Sister

M.H.M.

All here desire to be kindly remembered to you and yours—Write soon.

The Rutledge family was saddened by the news of General Thomas Pinckney's death on November 2, 1828. Few were left who remembered the War for Independence from firsthand knowledge.

A final letter from St. Petersburg, dated December 31, 1828, speaks of Septima's family and the touchy subject of Henry Middleton's return to America:

St Petersburg, Decr 31st 1828

After expecting many months to hear from you my dear Septima, your letter of the 15th of Septr reached me only a few days since, it gave me great pleasure. . . . You gave a good account of M^r R's health and Emma's, I hope I may conclude that your own was also benefitted by the excursion you mention & the subsequent healthy summer. By the time this reaches you I trust Mary will have recovered from her confinement, & you from your too anxious feelings concerning her, & that you may in consideration of this, & of Henrietta's happiness have become in some degree more reconciled to the afflicting dispensations under which you have suffered. Religion will lend its aid to enable you to support them. . . . You desire me to tell you my dear Septima when your Brother thinks of returning to America. If I were to ask him, I am sure he would give me an evasive answer, but from all that I can observe & judge from, I see no possibility of our leaving this country. . . . He & the rest of our circle unite with me in best love to you & yours & I am my dear Septima y^r affectionate

Sister

M.H.M.

Mary Helen and Henry Middleton left Russia in 1830. Henry Rutledge's friend, John Randolph of Roanoke, unadvisedly accepted President Jackson's appointment as the next minister to Russia. Ill health forced his premature return.

It was during 1828 that the Cherokee Indians, in north Georgia, published the *Cherokee Phoenix,* the first newspaper printed in a native Indian language. That spring, Noah Webster had published his first *American Dictionary of the English Language.* That same year Henry Rutledge, for the sum of one dollar, deeded part of his land, near Rose Hill, to Mary and Francis Fogg. The family was living there when Mary Fogg gave birth to a daughter, Septima Sexta Middleton Rutledge Fogg.

At this time the Foggs and the Rutledges were still much involved in organizing a Protestant Episcopal Church in Nashville. Their small number continued meeting at the Masonic Hall and included, as vestrymen Dr. John Shelby, Thomas Claiborne, James Stewart, and Henry Baldwin, Jr., as well as Francis Fogg.

December 22, 1828, found all of Nashville prepared to celebrate the election of their neighbor, Andrew Jackson, to the highest office in the land, president of the United States. Rejoicing quickly turned to sorrow as news of the death of Jackson's beloved Rachel spread through the town. Her funeral procession included Presbyterian elders as pallbearers, led by Governor Sam Houston. Major John Coffee and Henry Rutledge literally held Andrew Jackson as he walked toward Rachel's final resting place at the Hermitage. Services were held at 1:00 P.M. Christmas eve; thousands mourned with Jackson. Septima and Henry had been supported by Rachel and Andrew Jackson at the deaths of their children; an old bond had grown stronger with them.

Mary Fogg remembered and loved the way Rachel Jackson had befriended the Rutledge family—she also knew her brother, Edward, had found an additional family in the Jacksons and their nephew, Andrew Jackson Donelson. Mary immediately dispatched a personal note to their grieving friend, written inside a favorite book of hers. *The Mourner Comforted,* by James Abercrombie (Senior Assistant

Minister of Christ Episcopal Church in Philadelphia), was a collection of consolatory writings by the most eminent divines on the death of friends. Mary Fogg wrote:

> Let me request the honour of you my beloved old friend to accept this simple offering of a heart that *ever will be* most effectionately devoted to you, as it was warmly attached to the precious saint who has fled from us to the realms of purity & bliss; whose Christian excellencies it shall my delight to emulate until the last hours of life, in order that I may be forever united to her in the glorious presence of The Lamb of God. Let me request the honour of you my dear and honoured friend to read in the secret moment of repose from the high duties of your office, some of the words of consolation that flowed from the pen of one who knew the *utmost sorrow* & was "acqainted with grief." Let me assure my beloved Genl. that the most fervent & constant prayers for his peace & consolation are & *ever shall* be offered up by one who has drunk deep of the cup of affliction, but who anxiously is engaged for the future happiness of one she values so highly. Let me assure you then dear friend that I shall never cease to pray most fervently for your future & eternal happiness—Be so kind as to read particularly the Discourse marked by the Leaf turned down—

Genl. Andrew Jackson
In testimony of the profound
veneration & sincere affection
of his young friend
M. R. Fogg
1829

The following letter was his response:

Hermitage Janry 17th 1829

My Dear Madam
    I have received by the hand of our mutual friend Mrs. McLamare, the inestimable book which you were kind enough to present to me, to console me under my present affliction—I thank you kindly for this precious gift, & receive it as the highest evidence of your friendship, not only for me, but the dear partner & solace of my life, who providence has taken to that clime where the wicked disturb not, "and the weary are at rest."

Could this world compensate her loss, it might be found in the reflection, that her virtues, her piety & christianity, has ensured her that future happiness, which is promised to the desciples [sic] of Christ. The valuable book you have presented teach me, that the feeling of resignation to the dispensation of providence, is only the feeling of despair, when unsupported by his grace—that grace which has taken from me the dear partner of my bosom, and admonishes me by its sudden, solemn, & afflictive influence that I must soon follow her—your invaluable present will aid me in my preparation to unite with her in the realms above never to be seperated [sic]. I pray you to accept my sincere thanks for your kind present, with the assurance of my high respect, friendship & esteem.

Andrew Jackson

Mrs. Fogg

Nashville

On March 4, 1829, Andrew Jackson was inaugurated as the seventh president of the United States of America, with John C. Calhoun beginning his second term as vice-president. Jackson delivered his inaugural address in a low, almost inaudible, voice promising governmental economy, the protection of the rights of the states, certain reforms in the civil service, and just treatment for the Indians. Following the ceremony, such a large crowd gathered at the White House that refreshments were placed on the lawn to keep some of the people outside.

In Nashville, that same day, there was a dinner and program given at Vauxhall Garden to celebrate the inauguration of their President. Vauxhall Garden was a place of public entertainment established, in 1827, by Mr. Decker and Mr. Dyer. There was a ballroom and a large dining hall which could seat fifteen hundred for dinner. It was there, in 1832 and 1834, that President Jackson was honored by great receptions during his visits home.

Henry Rutledge was a favorite participant and speaker for patriotic events in Nashville, just as he had been in Charleston. The Rutledge children were often reminded of their heritage and that both of their grandfathers were signers of the Declaration of Independence. Ceremonies, on the Fourth of July, were much anticipated, especially by the young people.

On the eve of the decade of the 1830s, Andrew Jackson was the United States' President; Sam Houston had resigned as Governor of Tennessee due to tragic personal reasons, and the city of Nashville had begun to recognize the importance of its place in the nation.

Chapter Fourteen

In 1830, Henry Rutledge appeared on the census for both Franklin and Davidson counties in Tennessee. He and his son-in-law Francis Fogg were well-accepted members of the Davidson County bar. Henry Adolphus Rutledge, Henry's son, was following in the legal profession as well.

The coming of the thirties in Nashville saw marked improvements for the population of seven thousand. A reservoir and water system was completed, three hundred brick and two hundred frame homes lined the streets and avenues, and more than two hundred stores and shops were open for business. A newly erected courthouse, market house, post office, and city hall joined two large banking houses as well as a branch of the United States Bank.

The small Episcopal congregation, still meeting in the Masonic Hall in Nashville, formally organized under the name Christ Episcopal Church. By July 30, 1830, the cornerstone of this first Episcopal church building in Tennessee was laid at Spring and High Streets on the northeast corner. The year before, pews had been auctioned with none sold for less than fifty dollars. The very first bids were given by the families of Henry Rutledge and Francis Fogg. The highest bid was $182.00, paid by Mary and Francis Fogg.

In 1831, Septima Rutledge and Mary Fogg were part of the ladies society that purchased a church bell and organ in Philadelphia. Their zeal on behalf of their church was undaunted—their enthusiasm rarely equalled. This mother and daughter seemed to possess a unique spirit of cooperation reminiscent of the relationship shared by Septima and her own mother, Mary Izard Middleton.

On January 5, 1831, Dr. John Shelby resigned from the board of trustees of the University of Nashville; Henry Rutledge was elected to fill his post, joining Francis Fogg who had been a trustee since 1823. Henry continued in that capacity as a member in good standing until his death.

It was this educational link which provided Septima the determination and support needed to push for school funds for underprivileged children. Co-educational possibilities were nonexistent at that time, and her concern increased for young girls who were destitute or orphaned. She realized that children from disadvantaged situations had little or no opportunity for cultural exposure. Private schools or tutors were available only for those fortunate enough to possess ample means of payment. Septima and Mary discussed ways of alleviating this situation in Nashville with friends and faculty members within the University group.

In the beginning they were able to use Rose Hill as a base for an effort to reach young people who otherwise would have gone unschooled. Both mother and daughter influenced their husbands to begin legislative efforts to provide some form of public education. Important to that effort would be the early association of Francis Fogg with James Knox Polk when both were practicing law in Columbia, Tennessee.

Courtesy of Mary Stevenson Poling and Eleanor Stevenson Rutledge, Jacksonville, Ala.
Photo—Jim Wheeler

Christ Episcopal Church, Nashville, Tennessee, built 1830

Mrs. Polk, the former Sarah Childress of Murfreesboro, Tennessee, had received her education at Salem College in North Carolina and espoused the Moravian love of music. She, Septima, and Mary discussed the cultural void which existed for young girls in Nashville and urged other prominent women to help them organize classes. It would be several years before there would be any visible results of their efforts. They hoped there would be state legislation which would assure funding and local support for public schools.

General William Carroll, a native of Pennsylvania, was governor of Tennessee from 1821 to 1827 and from 1829 to 1835. A well-known merchant from Nashville, he owned the first hardware store and the first steamboat to reach that western outpost. Once a prominent figure in military ventures with Andrew Jackson, this people's candidate had broken with the "Hero of New Orleans" for reasons which were soon obscure. He became a new figurehead for democracy in the state, swept into office, and except for an inter-mission of one term, remained governor of Tennessee until 1835. He served longer than any governor in Tennessee history.

Of utmost importance to Governor Carroll was the establishment of a system of common schools for the state. As early as 1824, James K. Polk, as chairman of a joint committee, made a report to the legislature setting forth a plan to secure from Congress certain funds resulting from unappropriated land sales and to relinquish that money for the common school fund. Little progress was made even after Polk became a member of Congress. There was almost half a million dollars in this fund before the end of 1831, and yet there was still no effective system of public instruction. Some private academies offered assistance, but this was not the usual practice.

In 1833, Nashville merchants exported an estimated four and a half million dollars in cotton and tobacco. Besides river traffic, there was an increased demand for turnpikes, and the first maca-damized roads were constructed. The cultural standards of Virginia and the Carolinas were of great influence, and those families of standing in the community were responsible for the transformation of this western outpost into a civic metropolis.

Septima and Henry Rutledge were now very much a part of the growing cultural influence which caused increased civic awareness concerning both education and religion in Nashville. Their family members in South Carolina spoke of them with admiration. Visits from Henry's sister Sally were filled with the latest news of Henry and Mary Helen Middleton, other family members still living along the Ashley River, and as always news of Hampton Plantation on the South Santee.

So much of Sally's work now was with the orphanage in Charleston that she continued to encourage Septima to increase her charitable contributions in like manner there in Nashville. Septima and Mary Fogg urged the vestry of Christ Church to use the church building as a school for underprivileged children. In the meantime, Septima taught young girls from the Nashville area at Rose Hill, giving them the benefit of her own background in language and music.

These efforts culminated in the establishment of the Nashville Protestant School of Industry in 1837. The school was for orphaned or destitute girls and emphasized cultural studies and fine hand sewing skills. Septima's work had just begun, for she and her closest friends would now need to solicit the concern and support of numerous Nashville citizens in order to secure property and a building to house their school.

Chapter Fifteen

The era of arranged marriages was nearly over, but the importance of proper matches was still greatly emphasized. Septima and Henry's daughter Emma married Daniel Blake of South Carolina on June 8, 1831, in Nashville. This marriage once more united cousins, as Daniel Blake's mother was Septima's sister, Anna Louisa, who had married Daniel Blake, the second son of William and Anne Izard Blake. Anne Izard was the sister of Mary Izard Middleton, Septima and Louisa's mother. The Blakes had remained in England as Royalists during the American Revolution, receiving formal educations at Cambridge.

Emma's husband Daniel was born in England on January 31, 1803. In July of that year Daniel's grandfather, William Blake, died at his home Sunbury Place, County Middlesex, England. He had left his South Carolina plantations, Board House, and lands in

Courtesy of Mary Stevenson Poling and Eleanor Stevenson Rutledge, Jacksonville, Ala.
Photos—Jim Wheeler

Left—Henry Adolphus Rutledge (1805-1883). Right—Caroline Bell Nicholson Rutledge (1812-1878)

Savannah, Georgia, to his son Daniel. Therefore, this Daniel Blake, grandson of William Blake, was a wealthy low-country planter when he married Emma Middleton Rutledge.

Septima and Henry were pleased with the marriage, especially because Daniel Blake was a close associate of their son-in-law Frederick Rutledge. Septima knew Emma and Henrietta would see each other often in Charleston and that their husbands would provide them much security.

Another wedding for the Rutledge family took place on November 24, 1831. Twenty-six-year-old Henry Adolphus married Caroline Jane Bell Nicholson. She was known for her beauty and was referred to as the "Belle of Nashville." She was born April 12, 1812, and was a surviving twin who was raised by the McNairy's of Nashville after the death of her parents. Mrs. McNairy was Caroline's maternal aunt. Henry Adolphus and Caroline may have lived for a time at Rose Hill. She was baptized at Christ Episcopal Church in Nashville, October 21, 1832.

The next few years were filled with the promise of new life as Septima and Henry welcomed their grandchildren into this world. A name sake for Henry was born in 1831—Henry Middleton Rutledge Fogg—the third child of Mary and Francis. Emma and Daniel Blake's firstborn, Daniel Henry (named for both grandfathers), was born in Nashville and only lived from June 15 until August 13, 1832. On September 26 of that year, Henrietta and Frederick Rutledge had a daughter, Sarah Henrietta, to join two-year-old Elizabeth Pinckney, whom they called Lise. Henry Adolphus and Caroline Rutledge were the proud parents on August 6, 1833, of Emma Philadelphia, who was born in Nashville.

By the fall of 1834, the Rutledges of Chilhowee and Nashville were no longer pulled by thoughts of Charleston and Middleton Place. They were well established as necessary members of their community. Septima at fifty and Henry at fifty-eight had mourned the deaths of three children, had five still living, four of whom were married, and had six grandchildren.

On July 1, 1833, their sixteen-year-old son Arthur Middleton Rutledge received an appointment from Andrew Jackson to the military academy at West Point. Their son Henry Adolphus, with his wife and daughter, were embarking on a venture of their own. Henry had decided to practice law in Talladega County, Alabama, and to join others in the land speculation of the south. Their son-in-law Francis Fogg was a delegate to the state's 1834 Constitutional Convention and that same year was elected a state senator from Davidson County. Frederick Rutledge and Daniel Blake, their other two sons-in-law, had initiated the establishment of a summer colony in Flat Rock, North Carolina, which soon became known as the "Little Charleston of the Mountains."

Buncombe County (a portion of which became Henderson County), in western North Carolina, became accessible as a mountain resort for South Carolina low-country rice planters only after the completion of the Buncombe Turnpike in 1828. Prior to that time, Cherokee Indian braves had customarily brought their families to the cool mountain area, for the summer months, while they were on hunting expeditions. The turnpike, which followed the early Indian path to Ochlawaha (meaning muddy water) hence the name Mud Creek, was laid off from the ford of Cane Creek to the *flat rock* near the Blue Ridge.

It was 1829 when Frederick Rutledge, along with Judge Mitchell King and Charles Baring, first purchased land and began to promote the Flat Rock area as a possible resort for South Carolina aristocracy. The enthusiasm of these men helped overcome the handicap of travel—a trip to Europe, Rhode Island, or Saratoga Springs, New York was easy in comparison to a ten to fourteen day laborious journey to the "Land of the Sky." The difficulties in transporting families, slaves, livestock, etc., were manageable. The problem of bringing heavy furnishings for their mountain retreats was insurmountable in the beginning, yet even this was solved by the use of native walnut to make furniture in Flat Rock.

Peter A. Summey picked a site on Earl's Creek in 1830 to locate a mill which he ran for sixteen years. This mill became the location for a furniture factory producing tables, chairs, beds, and cabinets. This sturdy walnut furniture came into general use by the families of the summer people.

There was quite a contrast between local inhabitants of the Flat Rock area and its annual summer population. Slave labor and great wealth made the height of luxury possible for those on holiday, while the mountain natives had grown hardened to the task of deriving their livelihood from those hills. Tourism required economic adjustment. There was a certain rejection—a natural aversion to the intrusion of fancy clothes, classical music, and the formality of speech, religion, and manner which accompanied the low-country planters. The adjustment was gradual and was greatly aided by the permanent settlement of several families.

Daniel Blake, in his travels through Buncombe County and the Hoopers Creek Valley, became fascinated with the possibility of a comfortable summer home in the area of Limestone (once called Murrayville, afterwards known as Shufordsville, then Fletcher). He thought it an excellent location for a resort and soon began to help Frederick Rutledge promote the idea. In the winter of 1826, he spent several weeks at Murray's Inn on Cane Creek, originally stopping because of a lame horse, then remaining longer due to a snow storm. His fascination with the beauty of those peaceful surroundings caused him to purchase, from William Murray, some nine hundred and fifty acres, including the Inn, for a reported $10,000 in gold. The transaction was handled by his good friend Frederick Rutledge who purchased land in Flat Rock some three years later.

Extensive property in the Flat Rock area was purchased in 1830 and 1831 by Charles Baring, another wealthy South Carolina planter. He chose that particular location as a homesite for he and his wife Susan because of her health. Their home, Mountain Lodge, was built and landscaped following the typical pattern of the country seat in England. The grounds included an octagonal billiard house, a park, stocked with deer and other wild animals, surrounded by imported and native shrubs and trees. Mrs. Baring had been married five times before meeting Charles Baring in Philadelphia. It was no wonder that he spared no expense in the building of their North Carolina estate, part of which included a beautiful brick family chapel, known from earliest times as St. John in the Wilderness.

Courtesy of Baker/Barber Collection—Hendersonville, North Carolina

**St. John in the Wilderness Episcopal Church,
Flat Rock, North Carolina**

Courtesy—Kellwood Company, Asheville, North Carolina
Photos—Ray Neblett

Above—Widow's Watch in snowflake design, The Meadows, Fletcher, North Carolina. Below—The Meadows, Fletcher, North Carolina.

As the population of Flat Rock grew, so did the congregation of Episcopalians worshipping with the Baring family, so that in 1836, the Barings deeded to Bishop Ives their family chapel and a small nearby house, for the creation of a new parish. The original vestry included Daniel Blake, whose family had by that time settled in their home, The Meadows, built at Cane Creek on the old Murray Inn property.

There are many fascinating stories surrounding the lives of the Rutledge, Blake, and Baring families in this resort area of Western Carolina. The entertainment and living standards became lavish indeed. The Rutledge log house, built for summer use only, soon paled in comparison to Mountain Lodge (the Baring estate), Argyle (home of Judge Mitchell King), Saluda Cottages (home of Count Joseph Marie Gabriel St. Xavier de Choiseul, cousin of Louis-Philippe, King of France from 1830 to 1848), and Rock Hill (home of Christopher Gustavus Memminger).

The construction of the Blake home, as a permanent residence, gave Frederick and Henrietta Rutledge access to a lavish vacation home, while they maintained Hampton Plantation in South Carolina as their country seat. Henrietta's sister, Emma, delighted in having her family from Nashville and Charleston as guests for two or three months at a time. The Meadows, completed early in 1836, was built by a slave and his seven daughters. The masonry was skillfully handled, taking over two years to construct from limestone quarried on the property.

This two-story magnificent stone dwelling had two bay windows in the front and fourteen rooms, with ceilings which were fifteen feet high. The walls were thirty inches thick, and there were eight fireplaces, plus a widow's watch centered over the main stairwell, which peaked forty-five feet from the first floor. This widow's watch was designed in a snowflake pattern to symbolize the providential snow storm, in 1826, which accompanied the purchase of the Murray's Inn property and surrounding acreage by Daniel Blake.

At the top of the stairs, to the right, was one curved wall, which was a design feature of the period. This rounded corner provided a display area for sculpture and denoted the grandeur of the architectural style. Native woods of mahogany, black walnut, and cherry were used to magnificently frame the windows and towering oak doors.

Emma Rutledge Blake (1812-1852) standing and Henrietta Rutledge Rutledge (1807-1842) leaning. Portrait thought to be painted c. 1841-1842 by Samuel Osgood.

Photo—Ray Neblett

**Carriage entrance, St. John in the Wilderness Episcopal Church,
Flat Rock, North Carolina**

Hardy English boxwoods were used in the landscaping, and because of Emma Blake's passion for shades of lavender, her husband secured hyacinth and scilla bulbs, wisteria cuttings, and even wild flowers to accent the indigenous panorama with her favorite hue. Bricks, which had been used for ballast on ships coming from England, formed the flower bed borders and circular walkways.

Emma's religious background influenced her family's active participation as charter members of St. John in the Wilderness, though the trip to church on Sunday, southward to Flat Rock, involved a days journey round trip.

Emma Blake wrote poetry, reflecting on the loss of her first-born child and was at times melancholy, but she carried her mother's love of music and beauty to her Carolina mountain home. It was there in the wooded stillness that she raised her children and welcomed visits from her family. The Meadows and Flat Rock became a welcome place of retreat for the Rutledge family.

Chapter Sixteen

Henry's sister, Sally, and his stepmother had moved from Tradd Street to the north corner of Lamboll and Legaré Streets, in 1829. Septima was thankful she and Henry could travel to Charleston to be with Sally, for a time, following the death of Mrs. Rutledge on October 22, 1837. It was a time when all the family members in South Carolina really appreciated their presence.

In January of 1838, there was an interesting letter which mentioned Henry and Septima written by Mary Helen Middleton's daughter Eliza to her brother Henry in Paris. The "Russia" Middletons were much involved now in South Carolina life, following the time spent in St. Petersburg. Middleton Place reflected those years in Russia, with the display of the fine, full length portraits of Emperor Nicholas I and Empress Czarina Alexandra Feodorovna. The Emperor presented Henry Middleton these portraits because of his attachment to this American ambassador who remained in Russia for so many years (1820–1830).

Eliza, in her letter, describes the Christmas of 1837 and speaks of Septima and Henry's visit with the family at Middleton Place. Their daughters, Emma and Henrietta, were in Charleston, and so was Sally Rutledge. Septima and Henry were favorite visitors at Middleton Place.

> . . . But to return to our Xmas party. It was composed of Aunt & Uncle Rutledge, Daniel Blake and Lizzie Middleton (Pinckney's sister). The day after arrived Sarah, Joe & Arthur Huger . . . and the two Kings . . . We had also the Smiths from Runnymede which with our own party completed the 16 or 18 who sat down daily to dinner. Aunt R. (obliged to return to nurse 2 preg. daus. Emma & Henrietta) is a dear good soul, so affectionate and kind-hearted. She brought us each a little present. The little bouquet vase she gave me was the only one I received.

The letter referred to Septima's daughters who were expecting babies. Henrietta had had a third child, Edward, in April of 1836, and this fourth child was named Alice Izard. Emma had given birth on January 24, 1838, to a son, Frederick Rutledge Blake.

Courtesy—Middleton Place Foundation   Courtesy—Middleton Place Foundation

Mary Helen Hering Middleton   Henry Middleton (1770-1846)

Septima, therefore, had good reason to spend the winter and spring of 1838 in South Carolina. It was following her return to Chilhowee, for the summer, that word reached her of the fate of the steamship Pulaski, bound from Savannah, Georgia, to Baltimore, Maryland.

Within sight of the shore, just 150 miles north of Charleston, the vessel had exploded, killing countless friends and close relatives. The shipwreck occurred the evening of June 14 after the passengers had retired to their cabins. They had been enjoying dancing and music and unusually good weather as their annual trip north to Newport and Saratoga had begun. Most of the passengers were wealthy Georgia and South Carolina planters and their families. The ship's boiler had exploded, scattering parts of the vessel into the sea and causing the deaths of seventy-seven of the 131 passengers.

Frederick Rutledge lost his unmarried sister Maria Rutledge and his brother Thomas Pinckney Rutledge, who had just married Frances M. Blake, sister of Daniel Blake. Henrietta and Emma must have been heartbroken for their husbands in this overwhelming loss. Yet there was added sorrow for the entire family. Mary Helen and Henry Middleton's thirty-six-year-old daughter, Maria Henrietta, her husband, Edward Jenkins Pringle, and their children, all lost their lives on the Pulaski. The accounts of the struggle were frightful, relating how many clung to small boats or pieces of the wreckage, only to drown trying to reach the shore.

Septima grieved with her sons-in-law and her brother and Mary Helen to such an extent that she was unable to write their families in condolance for many weeks. She finally wrote the following letter to Mary Helen:

Chilhowee
18 Sept^r, 1838

Oh my Dearest Sister, how many Fruitless attempts have I made to write, & console with you on the Dreadful Event, which in Bereaving us of one of the Dearest Objects of our affection, has plunged us into so much affliction. The awful Tydings were so overwhelming, that for Weeks they entirely deprived me of the power of expressing all that I felt for you on the Occasion. For believe me my Loved Sister, y^r Sorrow was most truly mine, & Long, Long, shall I mourn the Angelic Creature, who is now I trust enjoying those Realms of Bliss & Peace to which her Nature was so Congenial. But for this perfect assurance of the Christian, my Dear Sister, how would it be possible to calm the Torturing feelings that assail us under such Deep Afflictions? Grief we know cannot Kill, or how few Mothers could Survive the Sad Trials to which they are subjected. I know by Sad experience, how Dreadful inspite of every effort, are our struggles against the Decrees of Fate; & how agonizing is the effect of so stunning a Blow, until Religion awakens us to Sense of our Duty to that Being on whose mercies we can only rely for aid, & who alone has power to heal the Wounds he Inflicts. For even when our murmurs cease, & we become more calm from a Conviction that they are unavailing, the wretched heart still too often sinks at the memory of Past Joys, & Life becomes truly a Burthen. This is the Sad Ordeal I too well know you must pass thro', my Dear Sister, . . . Altho' I know how unavailing is the Sympathy of Friends, mine would not have been withheld except from Necessity. Our long Tested Friendship forbids the thought, & it has been too often our Sad Task to endeavor to relieve each others Griefs, for my Silence to have been attributed to Neglect. For the impossibility of writing became the more painful from the anxiety I felt on y^r account. A letter to my Brother has no doubt ere this explained the cause. It was truly out of my power to offer you any Consolation . . . Many a Sleepless Night did I pass in dwelling on y^r Misfortune, which seemed almost too much for Human Nature to bear. God Grant that my apprehensions were groundless, & that you have gradually become more resigned to the Will of Heaven. The thought of the sad Chasm that the loss of this Charming little Circle will make in y^r happiness tho' is most aspiring; & the Image of my Lovely Niece is so associated with you all, that I cannot think of any of you without a Pang, . . . You have still many blessings left my Dear Sister, & many strong Ties to Life. And happly an Uncommon Constitution, which I trust will continue unimpaired. This has in truth been a [torn] melancholy Summer to us all, & how often have I wish'd that we could have passed it together. . . . I must now bid you Adieu! My Dear Sister, as I am still too Weak to write much. Let me hope that you will indulge me by letting me hear soon every particular relating to y^{r}self, & the Dear Circle in which I am so Deeply interested. My Children both near, & at a Distance, have all Sympathyzed most truly in y^r Affliction. They, & M^r R: unite with me in affect^{te} Remembrances to y^{r}self, my Dear Brother, & all around you, & believe me my Dear Sister

with much truth

y^r Sincerely attached

Sister

S:S:M:R:

There was much strength of faith evidenced by Septima's letters. Here was a woman who had known the personal tragedy of losing children—here was a woman who had struggled with depression and aloneness and uncertainties. Her own character had been formed around the strong conviction that God was in charge of all human history.

Her own health had at times been fragile, and yet she tirelessly spent what strength she possessed in the pursuit of benefits for others. Her own family members cherished her attention, her well-disciplined concern for them and their happiness. Beyond the family circle she reached out to aid those who were in need, ever mindful of the responsibilities she believed accompanied wealth and positions of influence.

A letter written in Nashville, December 22, 1838, to Mary Helen in Charleston, expressed once again Septima's source of strength and her obedient faith:

Nashville
Decr 22, 1838

What a relief it was to me to receive y^r letter my Dear Sister; altho' I could not help shedding many Tears over it. After all that I have suffered for you, I stood much in Need of the assurance that you were trying to bring y^r mind to a state of Resignation to be able to feel at all at ease about you. *That* is the only resource of the Christian in this Scene of Endless Trials, & Heaven Grant you Success. How often do we repeat, "Thy Will be done on Earth as it is in Heaven" & yet Venture to murmur at our Sad Fates. And it is only when our Hearts are torn by affliction that we feel the *full force* of all that we daily utter, as Evidences of our Submission to the Divine Will. All y^r strength of mind will be requisite, my Dear Sister, to bear up against y^r misfortune, & I wish with all my Heart that you could have gone immediately to Europe, instead of returning to Carolina, where every thing will renew y^r Grief for our loss, You will not tho' I hope remain much at M:P: [Middleton Place], for my Brother's business will of course oblige him to be a great deal away, & in Solitude, Grief is more apt to Prey upon the mind, . . .

Septima continued by telling Mary Helen how happy she was to know that Eliza would soon marry J. Francis Fisher. She speaks of Arthur's return from West Point where he received a commission as Second Lieutenant. She included family news, talked of Mary Fogg's bout with measles, mentioned the pleasure the Fogg's were experiencing in their new home across the street from Christ Church, then speaks of her own situation:

I had for several months much anxiety about my Dear Mary, who had a Violent illness in Sept^r, & was confined to her Bed for three Weeks, & reduced to such a State of Debility, (the Physicians say from the Effects of the Measles, & over Exertion) that she has not yet recovered her strength altho' Convalescent, & she is still confined to the House for fear of a return of Indisposition. She is so pleasantly situated now, that she did not mind being a Prisoner

During the Inclement Weather, & she has so many Kind Friends, that she will see as much of them as if she could visit them. The greatest recommendation to her charming Establishment is the Vicinity to the Little Church to which we both are so much attached, & we now pass every Sunday with her for the Convenience of going there. . . . Our situation is a Beautiful one tho' we ought to be reconciled to the Exile from our Native Home. . . .

She closed by remembering last Christmas with them at Middleton Place:

The approaching Season reminds me of the happiness I enjoyed near you all the Last Winter, & I dare not yet Dwell upon the Sad Change in that Dear Circle that I love so much. . . .

Septima confessed to Mary Helen her own difficulty in accepting their Tennessee "Exile" and yet admitted that their situation was a "Beautiful one." Her own efforts had brought much improvement to the society which surrounded her. It was indeed through her and her loved ones that the city of Nashville was responding to matters of civic importance.

Chapter Seventeen

Septima Rutledge maintained a closeness with her children even though their own lives carried them away from Rose Hill. Each grandchild was special to Septima and Henry. They could see that the family names were cherished and their line would be continued. Henrietta and Frederick Rutledge named their son, born August 5, 1839, Henry Middleton Rutledge. When news reached Nashville from Flat Rock, North Carolina, of his safe arrival and the name which he had been given, Henry's other namesake, eight-year-old Henry Middleton Rutledge Fogg, may have asked his mother if all the cousins would have the same names. His own sister and his new baby girl cousin in Alabama carried Septima's full name.

Henry Adolphus had moved to Talladega County, Alabama, shortly before the birth of his second child, Septima Sexta Middleton Rutledge. Seppie, as she was called, was born on February 3, 1836.

Her sister, Emma, was two years old at the time, and the girls' mother, Caroline, was determined to follow the example set by her mother-in-law in providing cultural advantages for her daughters.

The Rutledge plantation in Alabama was on land still surrounded by Indians. It was not unusual for Caroline to be busy with her children, only to notice that she was being watched by an Indian in full native dress. She was anxious over this lack of privacy and asked her husband to question the Indians, as he understood their language. They explained to him that they thought she was a spirit and that they only wanted to watch her and the children. This was not enough reassurance, so at Caroline's insistence they moved back to Nashville until the Indians were sent to the reservation. By 1839, Henry Adolphus, Caroline, Emma, and Seppie had returned to Talladega, where they lived in town so Henry could resume his law practice.

In 1840 one of Septima's dreams for Nashville became reality. The school for girls, which she and Mary had helped to organize in 1837, was given a plot of ground on Vine Street just above Spring Street. Mr. Joseph Elliston donated the land and had a modest house built there. He turned the deed over to the ladies under a board of managers headed by Mrs. James K. Polk. It was popularly called the House of Industry and was governed by the following law:

Section 1. Be it enacted by the General Assembly of the State of Tennessee, that the school for the support and education of destitute girls, now in existence and operation in the city of Nashville, be, and the same is hereby, incorporated under the name of the Nashville Protestant School of Industry for the education and support of destitute girls; and have perpetual succession. That it have the right to sue and be subjected to suit; make all by-laws necessary for the government of said school, take and hold real estate for the erection of suitable buildings, and take personal property by gift or otherwise, and to do all other acts necessary and within the scope of the benevolent objects of said institution.

Sec. 2. That the school and institute be under the control and direction of twelve Trustees, seven of whom shall be authorized to

House of Industry, Nashville, Tennessee

transact the business and have control of said school; and in case of vacancy it may be filled by the Board aforesaid. The present Board of Trustees shall be Mrs. Francis B. Fogg, Mrs. H. M. Rutledge, Mrs. Thomas Maney, Mrs. A. V. Brown, Mrs. G. W. Martin, Mrs. D. McGavock, Mrs. G. W. Campbell, Mrs. James Porter, Mrs. H. H. McEwen, Mrs. Washington Barrow, Mrs. H. Kirkman, and Mrs. O. Ewing, who may elect all necessary officers, teachers, and servants.

Sec. 3. That the destitute girls who are or shall become pupils in said school shall be under the control and guardianship of said Board of Trustees, who shall have the custody and care of the persons of said children, and exercise all the rights and duties of guardians, and bring suits for wrongs done, and recover the custody of their persons in the name of said school; and said guardianship shall be from the period of time when said pupils shall enter said school.

It was exclusively a working-girls home, and every girl who was admitted had to be either orphaned or abandoned, sound of mind and body, and eager to take complete responsibility for the upkeep, cleaning, and care of the home. The older girls were taught fine sewing and supported the younger girls with their dressmaking skills.

The rules for contact with the outside world were very strict, just as they were in the private homes of the trustees. These girls were given cultural and educational advantages, so that they would someday make suitable wives. Quite a few girls from the House of Industry entered marriages of affluence. The managers and trustees could proudly cite the records of the girls and their subsequent lives, knowing there had been much accomplished.

It was during the early forties that Septima and Mary came to equate charity with its true meaning—love. They were happy in their work with the girls at the House of Industry, and Mary's twelve-year-old daughter, Septima Fogg, often accompanied her mother and grandmother to the school. The three of them arranged musicals and outings, helped with French lessons, and at times walked to services with those girls who chose Christ Church as their place of worship.

On September 19, 1841, Septima Fogg and her brother Francis Fogg, Jr., were confirmed at Christ Church in Nashville. The teachings of the church held very special meaning for Mary Fogg's daughter. She had accompanied her grandmother to Flat Rock, North Carolina, the preceding summer for the baptism of her cousins Daniel Francis Blake and Emma Fredericka Rutledge. The service was performed July 31, 1841, by the Reverend Thomas S. W. Mott, rector of St. John in the Wilderness Episcopal Church. The two Septimas were witnesses and mentioned as such in the parish records. It was a joyful occasion and must have touched young Septima. She became more fervent in her participation at Christ Church, often singing solos for special services. She practiced, in coloratura range, the sacred selections accompanied by her grandmother. As Septima played the harp, the generation between her and her namesake must have seemed insignificant. Sweet melody erased what differences there might have been and the memory of their hours together would linger long after the music stilled.

Chapter Eighteen

In September of 1842, Henrietta Rutledge, the charming, beautiful daughter, wife, and mother who was fond of wearing a red rose in her hair and humming lullabies to her babies, died of a heart attack at The Meadows near her beloved Flat Rock, North Carolina. Her husband Frederick, having studied medicine, knew he was helpless in his efforts to revive her. He was unable to fathom the loss of his dearest treasure. Henrietta's sister Emma mourned so deeply that her husband Daniel feared for her health. The once happy clan, which had gathered at their summer colony in Western Carolina, now filed past Henrietta's coffin in shocked disbelief.

Mrs. Susan Baring of Mountain Lodge in Flat Rock had been in poor health and was evidently obsessed with the arrangements for her own funeral. Family tradition records that she

. . . had an English coachman and in her stables were four black horses that she'd had well trained. Mrs. Baring also had a black velvet pall, embroidered in silver, as she believed that if she must live and die in the wilderness, she would have a funeral befitting her present station. "Les pompes funèbres" were scarce in North Carolina. Upon hearing of Mrs. Rutledge's sad and sudden death, Mrs. Baring offered the horses with their black plumes, the pall, and the coachman, which the family accepted. The carriage was either taken off the springs, or an ordinary wagon used, as there was no hearse available. As was customary, the women did not attend the interment; the men of the family and their friends rode sorrowfully with Henrietta's body to Flat Rock. They were met at Taber's Hill by the cousins and friends who lived in that community and accompanied the coffin to the churchyard. . . . In that time, Charleston was at least two weeks away from Flat Rock and Fletcher, even for mail. A cousin . . . appeared at breakfast one morning, very pale and sad, saying she had had unhappy dreams, and was convinced something terrible had happened in North Carolina. She remembered the dream vividly and told it, describing the four horses driven by a white coachman in black livery, drawing a wagon containing a box covered with a black and silver cloth.

It was followed by a procession of men carrying their black hats in their right hand and being quietly joined by an equally quiet group, also hatless, at Taber's Hill.

Never had that mountain wilderness witnessed such deep Victorian mourning. The little girls never forgot having to wear black crepe pantalettes, instead of lace, buttoned on to their white drawers. The little boys wore black arm bands as a sign of sorrow at the death of their pretty mother.

Frederick Rutledge arranged for Lise, Sarah Henrietta, and Edward to return to Hampton plantation. There his mother, Harriott Pinckney Horry Rutledge, would care for those three of Frederick's children while the youngest three, four-year-old Alice Izard, three-year-old Henry Middleton, and one-and-a-half-year-old Emma Fredericka (she was called Minna) were taken to their maternal grandmother, Septima, and their Aunt Mary in Nashville.

Emma Blake's daughter, Frances Caroline Helen, had been born August 13 and baptized by Reverend Mott on September 19 just a few days before Henrietta died. This, plus the birth of another daughter, Henrietta Louisa, the following year, left Emma drained physically and emotionally. She was unable to help Frederick Rutledge with her sister's children; she was unable to go to her mother and father in Nashville; she was, in fact, seriously depressed and withdrawn at times. Her only outlet was her poetry and her visits to her sister's lonely grave next to St. John in the Wilderness Church.

Alice Izard, Henry Middleton, and Minna brought renewed purpose and life to Rose Hill. The cherry orchard and terraced gardens welcomed the addition of Septima's young grandchildren; the double parlors and music room at Rose Hill resounded once again with lilting cherubic laughter; the spacious kitchen acknowledged the toddlers' presence with the once familiar aroma of tea cakes and steamed puddings; the house itself seemed to embrace Henrietta's children with memory and warmth.

By Christmas of 1843, the little ones were quite well adjusted to their new life. Septima and Henry were satisfied with the care of the other three children at Hampton plantation and felt that Frederick Rutledge had made a wise decision.

In Nashville, the new year of 1844 was greeted with enthusiasm by the Rutledge and Fogg families. There had been no plan to winter in Charleston or Philadelphia—after all there were children once again—and their lives needed the stability of a full year's cycle in their new home.

Septima had grown to love the changing seasons in Tennessee. The drama which unfolded reminded her of the Resurrection. Winter's stillness was filled with anticipation, a waiting for the certain dependable arrival of spring—new life.

With the presence at Rose Hill of such little ones there emerged the painful memories of Septima's youngest children. Helen had been four and Cotesworth Pinckney only two at the time of their deaths, some sixteen years earlier. Caring for these grandchildren would be a reminder of that loss. It would also be a chance for fulfillment of plans and dreams Septima had thought gone forever.

Henry Rutledge was happy to see Septima enjoying the children. His dark gray Rutledge eyes twinkled as Alice, Henry, and Minna gathered around him for good night stories. He too remembered the sounds of child-like joy which once filled Rose Hill—he often thought about Henrietta—how she had loved her younger brother and sister and had grieved at their deaths; how she had loved her own children; how she had wanted to insure happiness for her little clan and a knowledge of their heritage.

Septima and Henry would often take their three wards to the Fogg home at the corner of Spring and High, across the street from Christ Church, for the weekend. It was a fine large home, and Mary's children, Septima and Henry, enjoyed the company of their cousins. Francis Fogg, Jr., had graduated from the University of Nashville, in 1843, and was now studying at Cambridge Law School.

It was during just such a weekend visit, on Saturday January 20, 1844, when Henry Rutledge, at the age of sixty-eight, suddenly became ill and by midnight was dead. Septima was at his bedside, as were Mary and Francis. Henry's death was unexpected, his family quite unprepared for the devastating loss, and the entire city of

Nashville stunned to read in *The Republican Banner* on Monday, January 22, the following:

> Death of Major Rutledge. Died in this city on Saturday last, the 20th inst., about midnight, very suddenly. Major Henry M. Rutledge, the only son of Hon. Edward Rutledge, one of the signers of the Declaration of Independence. . . . One of the purest lights and brightest ornaments of our society is extinguished . . . He filled many situations of honor, in all of which his integrity of heart and soundness of understanding were strikingly exhibited. To a dignity of mind and character worthy of his illustrious lineage he added the most polished taste and the most genuine and enlightened benevolence. Far from the gaze of the multitude and the frivolous agitations of this bustling life, he spent many an hour in visiting the poor and distressed, and pouring into the wounded hearts of widows and orphans the balm of consolation and comfort; and many an humble but aspiring student has had the benefit of his purse, as well as of his counsel and direction. . . . Major Rutledge died at the residence of his son-in-law, Francis B. Fogg, Esq. The funeral will take place this afternoon at 3 o'clock from the Episcopal Church; Services by the Rev. J. T. Wheat.

The legislature adjourned for the funeral, and despite inclement weather, a large crowd gathered at Christ Church for the services.

Funeral customs since the turn of the century still followed a resolution of the Continental Congress which required that:

> On the death of any relation or friend, none of us, or nay of our families, will go into any further mourning dress, than a black cape or ribbon on the arm or hat for gentlemen, and a black ribbon necklace for the ladies, and we will discontinue the giving of gloves and scarfs at funerals.

This tradition originated with the boycot of British goods and of course continued as practical in the West. The servants were given special duties in connection with funerals. The black women, who were called Waiters, numbered between two and six, and were dressed in white with a black scarf over the shoulder which reached to the knees. These Waiters were present at the house and carried silver trays with sprigs of Rosemary, for remembrance, which they gave each invited guest. These sprigs were carried to the cemetery and cast on the coffin, before the grave was filled with earth. The

Waiters walked in front of the cortege. Friends of the family sent their carriages for the ladies and children who rode behind the hearse. The pallbearers walked on each side of the hearse, and the gentlemen friends walked in procession along the walkways.

At the home of the deceased, all blinds were closed, the shades pulled, and the servants dressed in black. The pallbearers wore hats trimmed with a scarf of crepe, tied in a knot in back with streamers about one-half yard long, black silk arm bands, and black gloves. The women and girls wore hoods of black silk over their bonnets. These hoods draped to the eyes in front and were doubled up and sewn in back, so as to separate at the neck. Following the interments, there was a meal served which included the customary burnt wine. Families were large and funerals such a part of their lives that the articles of mourning were kept in a special chest in readiness when needed.

When Henry Rutledge died, he was sixty-eight years old and the grandfather of fifteen. At his death mourners came from Franklin and Coffee Counties in Tennessee, as well as those in the vicinity of Davidson County and Nashville. In the weeks that followed his burial, there was a steady stream of visitors from North and South Carolina, Georgia, Alabama, and Kentucky, not to mention messages from other states and eventually from friends and family in Europe.

Francis Fogg and his brother Godfrey initiated proceedings for the probating of Henry's will and helped Septima with other business matters. The will was recorded February 5, 1844:

I Henry Middleton Rutledge of the County of Davidson & State of Tennessee being (and I believe) of sound & disposing mind do make, publish & declare this to be my last Will & Testament in manner & form following to wit

Whereas previous to my marriage with my wife Septima Sexta Middleton she was possessed in her own right of certain negro Slaves to the number of ninety nine . . .a certain plantation or tract of land in the Parish of St. George (Dorchester) in South Carolina . . . in the event of the said Septima Sexta being the Survivor she will be entitled to receive the sum of thirty thousand four hundred & ten dollars out of my Estate in preference to other claims . . . I hereby declare that all of the Slaves in my possession in the State with the exception of Carpenter John and Sawyer (whom however

I hereby devise to my wife) and some other Slaves now in the possession of my Son Henry in Alabama are the remaining Slaves for
their descendents enumerated in the deed of Trust as aforesaid, and
it is further my will & intention that should my wife wish to continue planting at Chilhowee or on any other tract she may do so; a
convenient quantity of Land being laid off for her benefit during
the term of her natural life. And I do hereby give and bequeath to
her . . . all of the furniture plate & household articles together with
the horses and carriages I may have at the time of my death. But
my Books I wish divided between my Sons Henry & Arthur & the
papers not necessary to the settlement of my Estate or relating to
the same I wish to be delivered to Henry. I further give and devise
to my said wife the house & grounds where we reside in the vicinity
of Nashville. . . amounting to about twenty acres . . . I hereby
bequeath to my Son Arthur Middleton all the Lands . . . in the
Counties of Franklin & Coffee to him & his heirs forever and the
rest & residue of my Estate . . . to my daughters Mary & Emma
intermarried with Francis B. Fogg & Daniel Blake Esquires & to
my son Arthur M. Rutledge & the children of my late daughter
Henrietta who was intermarried with Frederick Rutledge Esq of
Charleston, S.C. to them & their heirs forever. . . .

H.M.Rutledge

P.S. I think proper to state my reason for not making any further
devise to my Son Henry than a portion of my Books & papers. . . .
I have conveyed to him at different times Land equal to his portion
& have assisted him with money in purchasing property. . . . Under
this impression I have not thought it right to make any further
provision for him.

H.M.R.—

Henry's most important consideration had been security for
Septima. He provided for the settlement of any debts and justly
divided the remainder among his children and Henrietta's heirs.

This quiet, dignified son of Edward Rutledge had by his life
helped to answer the now silent call of those signers of America's
Declaration of Independence to "preserve us a nation." His enter-
prise in the westward movement had extended the cultural influence
of the colonies and had brought with it a sense of the vital need for
education as well as material expansion.

That same year, 1844, Samuel F. B. Morse tested his invention, the telegraph, by sending the first message from Washington, D. C., to Baltimore, Maryland—it simply asked, "What hath God wrought?" One answer could well have been that God had wrought, into the mainstream of America, the dedicated perseverance and exemplary character of such men as Henry Middleton Rutledge.

Chapter Nineteen

Those years following Henry's death were for Septima a time of testing. Her three young grandchildren were a joy to her; yet their education and care were constant challenges. At the proper time she knew that Mary would assume the responsibility for their schooling.

The presence of Henrietta's children at Rose Hill reemphasized to Septima the need for an orphanage in Nashville. In February 1845, Septima, Mary, and numerous other prominent women of Nashville, met at the First Presbyterian Church to organize the Nashville Protestant Orphan Asylum. Mary Fogg was elected vice-president of the Board of Managers, and she and her mother gave continued support to that philanthropic institution. They began with a small rented house in south Nashville and one little girl, and before the end of the first year there were eighteen children. By 1847, the Board of Managers purchased from Mr. Francis McGavock a house and lot on McLemore Street. The women secured donations and fully subscribed the underwriting of expenses until 1848. At that time the County Court granted an allowance of twenty dollars a year per child under seven. This was later increased to thirty dollars per year without regard to age.

The Board employed a lady teacher. Regular school hours were observed, as well as "Sabbath-school." Household duties were taught the children, and they were placed in homes when possible so they would have parental love. They were only asked for "obedience and filial regard" in return.

On December 7, 1844, Tennessean James Knox Polk was elected president of the United States, and at the Hermitage near Nashville, on June 8, 1845, Andrew Jackson followed his beloved Rachel in death.

On July 4, 1845, the cornerstone was laid for the Tennessee State Capitol building, a magnificent edifice designed by architect William Strickland. The capital city of Nashville was the center of river traffic as well as a network of roads leading into all areas of the state and the most distant parts of the Union. Stage lines brought large numbers of visitors, plus the daily mail pouches, which kept the local newspapers more current than ever before. The citizens, as a result, were better informed, and the world outside seemed far less remote. By 1847, the Nashville papers carried the following advertisement:

> Leaving Nashville to Dalton, Ga., via Chattanooga, three times a week, making the trip through in 44 hours and returning to Nashville in 40 hours. The proprietor has at great trouble and expense, completed the arrangement for through tickets to Charleston from Nashville for $22, to Augusta $18, to Atlanta $13, and to Dalton for $12. The line leaves the Nashville Inn Mondays, Wednesdays and Fridays at 8 P.M., where through tickets may be had, and in Murfreesboro at Lytle's Hotel, and from Dalton to Nashville returning leaving Dalton on Tuesdays, Thursdays and Saturdays. Time from Nashville to Charleston 3½ days, to Augusta 3 days, to Atlanta 2½ days, from Nashville to New York via Charleston in 6 days, being two days less time than the same place can be made by any other route. . . . The proprietor would respectfully ask of the travelling public to give his line a trial, as he can assure them that it is by 24 hours the quickest one from Nashville to Charleston, and in the saving of time offers greater inducements to the travellers East than any other.

The year 1847 marked the first publication of *The Carolina Housewife, or House and Home,* written and compiled by Miss Sarah Rutledge. Cousin Sally featured in her book various Carolina menu attractions, plus European recipes or "receipts" which reflected her own education and travels with the Thomas and Charles Cotesworth

Pinckney families. There were additional items contributed by friends who had taken the "Grand Tour" and by those who served as envoys in the various countries. No doubt Mary Helen Middleton had shared in the Russian entries. Specific states, and even plantations such as Hampton, were given credit for receipts. The reader was encouraged to try the Indian's *Seminole Soup* and several dishes featuring cooters (turtles), a Jamaican favorite.

The family was very happy that Sally had published her book. It contained bits of Charlestonian custom not recorded elsewhere. Septima knew that Sally herself was no cook, which made her selections all the more interesting. Her written instructions covered everything from "a simple method of making nice cream cheese," to the gourmet details of "How to dress a calfs head in imitation of turtle." Rice dishes such as *Hopping John* and *Carolina Pilau,* plus treats made with flour were included along with *Okra Soup, Ragout of Pigeons, Shrimp Pie, Saluda Cornbread, Pamona Jelly, Raspberry Charlotte,* and many, many other culinary delights. Miss Rutledge covered household hints and cures as well, making this little volume extremely significant in the years to follow.

Septima continued contact with Sally Rutledge and Mary Helen Middleton through the long years away from Charleston. She drew comfort from her close association with them as they intimately shared their griefs and joys.

Mary Helen became a widow just two years after Septima. Governor Henry Middleton, of Middleton Place, died in Charleston June 14, 1846, and was given a public funeral with all military honors. Not long after her brother's death, Septima became quite ill herself. At sixty-three she was experiencing some problem with severe arthritis and, at one point, may have suffered a slight stroke or heart attack. She returned to Chilhowee and its nearby spring for cure and restoration. From there she wrote the following letter to Mary Helen who was at The Morris House in Philadelphia visiting her daughter Eliza Middleton Fisher.

Chilhowee

Octr 28th 1847

Judging by the unchangeableness of my own Nature my Dear
Sister, I cannot doubt that it will give you not a *little* pleasure to
learn that my *probation* has once more past, & my Heart again
vibrates with its Usual warmth of affection, & Yearns for the Comfort of Friendship, & the renewal of a Correspondence which for
the last 46 years of our Lives has never been interrupted, except
from Dire Necessity. How often did I think of y^r kind caution on
the Subject of *Health*, when too late. But the fact is, . . . I neglected
the study of the *Water Cure*, under the impression that I should
not require it; & made the Book a Present to one who I thought might
Benefit from it. I then had recourse to *Galvanic Belts & Rings*, &
all the New experiments without effect as I had no *Faith* in any
Remedy. I . . . lost all my Energy, & became such a Sufferer that
but for my Dear Arthur's resolution in insisting upon my returning to
the Cumberland Mountains, I could not possibly have Survived, as the
Physician thought that the attack was so Violent that there was little
Hope of recovery. And my restoration at length proved so Lingering,
that I could not risk the Journey of two Hundred miles further, to pass
the Remainder of the Summer with my Dear Emma, for which she was
most anxious, & thus I was deprived of the pleasure also of being near,
Dear Lise, & her Father, who always on these Occasions has made the
kindest, & most attentive Nurse & Physician, & to my great regret I
was prevented gratifying them with a sight of the three Dear Children,
who have been so long the Objects of our tenderest care. . . . I truly
lamented being the cause of detaining my Children at a Place
where there was no attraction except for Invalids, but they readily
forgot the sacrifice, & thought only of the benefit I might receive. . . .
Dear Mary remained with me for two months, . . . I had reason to
regret tho' that the fatigue she underwent in her Labors as a Souer
de Charité prevented her from profitting by the Delightful Climate.
The Scenery around the Springs is Extensive, & Beautiful, compre-
hending at one view 8 *Counties*, & the Various ranges of Mountains running thro' them. And from one Point we coud see *Chattanooga*, the Terminus of the Georgia *Rail Road*, now so *noted* as it
is to unite the South with the West . . . it is thought will be a great
advantage to these States. On the Summit of the Mountains from
which there is a very fine View, there is also a Garden, prettily
arranged, & is filled with the most Luxuriant Shrubs & Flowers
which often tempted me to make an Exertion to walk, & enjoy

their Fragrances. . . . The Springs that particularly of Calibiate [sic] is said to be the strongest on the Mountain, & performs really wonderful Cures, & if they were in good hands, they would be almost Desirable resort. But in their present State of discomfort, nothing but Necessity Induces any one to visit them . . . . We at least had ½ dozen Families from Nashville, who often visited us & among them my Friend M.rs Judge Campbelle & her Daughter. . . . She often enquires with Interest after you. . . . Then my sweet little charges put to School, & left them under the care of their Aunt Mary, & then stayed but a fortnight in Nashville, as the repairs making to our House, in which Painting was included affected me so much, that I came here for a Purer Atmosphere, & as my Dearest Arthur's improvements in the way of Mills, . . . will afford him full occupation for some Weeks, the least return I can make for his Filial devotion is not to leave him alone, but remain until his business is over, & my Sweet little Grand Daughter Emma will divide our Solitude with us: My Son Henry brought her to me accompanied by the rest of his Family, & after making visit of a Week only, was obliged by an Urgent Law suit to return to Alabama. My Daughter Caroline it grieved me to find in very Delicate Health, but I trust that a visit to New Orleans in the Winter will be the means of restoring her. You cannot think how impatient I am to hear from you again, my Dear Sister, for you are particularly associated with my earliest Scenes of happiness, & still Cling to the Remembrance of the affections of the Past, as the Greenest Spots of my life. Alas! how sad the change that, a few years have made in the Situation of all. Now I feel most Keenly that, "many Fatal recollections, many Sorrows, throw their Bleak shade alike oer my Joys & my Woes." But we are only Sojourners here. . . . Pray let me hear from you, & of all yr Family. After so long an *absence* as it seems to me, & the silence of all my Correspondents, . . . I am desirous of knowing where, & how, you all got thro' the Summer, & where you will pass the Winter. When did my Nephew Arthur leave you with his Family? I truly regretted his not succeeding in getting an appointment, & that he would not allow me to try any influence with the President's *Lady*, who is quite a Favorite of Mine. I shall have another Friend at Washington this winter, who went a few Years ago, as Minister to Portugal, & now goes to Washington as member of Congress. I might request his application if there should occur an opening for any Suitable Situation, for he has the highest Estimation of my Nephew's Reputation as a Diplomatist; of which he heard from an English Gentleman, who was one of the Legation of *Spain* was well acquainted with Arthur, & thought so highly of the Distinguished Character that he had maintained at *that* Court, that I am sure Genl Barrow will be a very warm advocate in his Favor. . . . How sad, & Various are the Warnings that we are constantly receiving to be thankful for the blessings granted us! Should you see my good Sister Miss Rutledge, on her way to Carolina, pray tell her the cause of my long silence, & with my Love, say that the Fear of my letters missing her induced me to Direct to Charleston, where I shall hope it will find her safely returned from her Summers Excursion. You must as usual excuse my long Garrulous Epistle, & with Love to every Member of Y^r Family, & kind remembrances to all Enquiring Friends, in both which request my Son Arthur most Cordially Joins, believe ever

Y^r attached Sister,

S.S.M.R.

Septima's recovery and subsequent return to Nashville gave credence to her own words, her steadfast belief "that we are . . . to be thankful for the blessings granted us." She viewed herself and all others as "only Sojourners here" and endeavored to reach out in compassion, not only to family and friends, but to those who were less fortunate, less equipped to endure life's trials, less able to rejoice at the beauty of creation due to hardship. Her awareness of suffering was not a casual observation, not a token charitable whim, but rather a magnificent shared journey of the spirit inspired by the unbroken chain of love she embraced for herself and all those within the sphere of her "dear Circle." Years later, her own great-grandson Archibald Rutledge, poet laureate of South Carolina, may have said it best—"A life without a generous and consuming enthusiasm is a dead life."

Being fully alive remained the ultimate challenge, the highest expression of the glory of God, and the supreme legacy to be claimed by the generations that followed Septima Sexta Middleton Rutledge.

Part VI

SEPTIMA

(1845-1865)

Mary Middleton Rutledge - Francis Brinley Fogg
(1801-1872)   M. 1823   (1795-1880)

Francis Brinley Fogg Jr. (1825-1848)

Septima Sexta Middleton Rutledge Fogg (1828-1851)

Henry Middleton Rutledge Fogg (1831-1862)

Henry Adolphus Rutledge - Caroline Jane Bell Nicholson
(1805-1883)   M. 1831   (1812-1878)

Emma Philadelphia Rutledge (1833-1863)

Septima Sexta Middleton Rutledge (1836-1920)

Henrietta Middleton Rutledge - Frederick Rutledge
(1807-1842)   M. 1825   (1800-1884)

Elizabeth Pinckney Rutledge (1830-1912)

Sarah Henrietta Rutledge (1832-1906)

Edward Rutledge (1836-1856)

Alice Izard Rutledge (1838-1854)

Henry Middleton Rutledge (1839-1921)

Emma Fredericka Rutledge (1841-1919)

Emma Middleton Rutledge - Daniel Blake
(1812-1852)   M. 1831   (1803-1873)

Daniel Henry Blake (1832-1832)

Frederick Rutledge Blake (1838-1907)

Daniel Francis Blake (1841-1872)

Frances Caroline Helen Blake (1842-1920)

Henrietta Louisa Blake (1843-1873)

Arthur Middleton Blake (1848-   )

Henry Middleton Rutledge Blake (1851-1856)

Arthur Middleton Rutledge - Eliza "Light" Underwood
(1817-1876)   M. 1851   (1829-1865)

Elizabeth Underwood Rutledge (1852-1918)

Emma Blake Rutledge (1854-1940)

Arthur Middleton Rutledge, Jr. (1855-1933)

Joseph Underwood Rutledge (1859-1876)

Genealogy VI—Septima (1845-1865)

Chapter Twenty

Septima Rutledge outlived Henry by twenty-one years, Mary Helen (who died May 24, 1850) by fifteen years, and Cousin Sally (who died April 13, 1855) by ten years. Her life spanned that period of American history from the close of the Revolution against the British to the desolate finish of the War Between the States.

Septima's death, on June 12, 1865, came only six days following the release of Confederate prisoners of war by President Andrew Johnson. On the twenty-second of February that same year her beloved Middleton Place had been burned by Federal troops under the order of William Tecumseh Sherman on his relentless "march to the sea." By the fifteenth day of April, 1865, Abraham Lincoln had been assasinated. Nashville, Tennessee, was occupied by Union soldiers from February 25, 1862 until the close of the war.

Septima's will, written January 15, 1864, declared the uneasiness of the times:

> The following is my last Will & Testament—In consequence of the disturbed condition of the country and the uncertain value of property, I revoke all former wills. . . . I direct my executor hereinafter named to sell all of my real estate upon credit or upon such terms and conditions as he may deem expedient and out of the proceeds he will first pay any debts that I may owe—then Five hundred dollars to Mary Nichol daughter of my friend Sarah Nichol and the remainder is to be distributed in equal shares as follows, towit: One fifth to the children of my deceased daughter Emma Blake. One fifth to the children of my deceased daughter Henrietta Rutledge. One fifth to my daughter Mary Fogg wife of Francis B. Fogg. One fifth to my son Henry Rutledge for life with remainder to his children and one fifth to my son Arthur M. Rutledge for life with remainder to his children. The portions here given to Henry Rutledge and Arthur M. Rutledge for their lives, with remainder to their children respectively, are to be vested in goods, public stocks or in notes secured by mortgages or real estate before distribution by my executor.

December 15, 1864, was the beginning of the two day Battle of Nashville, cited by some as the last major conflict of the war.

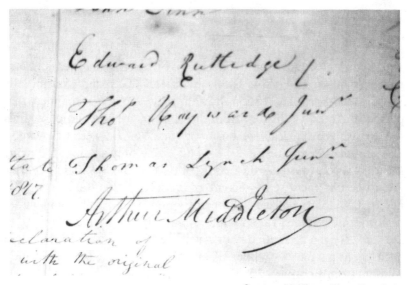

Signatures, South Carolina signers, Declaration of Independence.

One-half of a stereoscopic pair showing main house and north wing after they were burned in 1865.

Septima must have felt relief that Henry was not alive to witness the grief and destruction war had brought to Nashville and to Charleston. Could this really be the same country for which their fathers helped declare independence? Could Arthur Middleton and Edward Rutledge possibly have foreseen a future struggle that would involve their grandsons and great-grandsons.

The War for Independence, with its momentous signing of the colonies' declaration in 1776; its years of battle during which both of those refined patriots were imprisoned in a British-occupied Florida dungeon; its glorious cause, defended by resourceful allies such as Lafayette and DeKalb; that war's pains of labor should have ended by heralding the birth of a strong infant nation. That must have been Septima's conclusion: an infant nation, a mere baby with its growing years still ahead, could be nurtured to maturity only through pain, and brokeness, and finally healing. Septima and Henry had seen that to be true in their own lives and in the lives of their children.

Mary and Francis Fogg lost all three of their children during Septima's lifetime. Their oldest, Francis Brinley, Jr., died very suddenly on February 12, 1848, of inflamation of the brain. His death at age twenty-two came on the evening before he was to marry a Miss Martin of Nashville.

Three years later Septima Fogg died at age twenty-three. Her death on October 26, 1851, was caused by consumption. Her friends noted how rapidly she declined and how her beautiful voice would be missed at Christ Church by the music lovers of Nashville.

The Fogg's third child, Henry Middleton Rutledge Fogg, died, when only thirty-one, of wounds received at the Battle of Fishing Creek at Mill Springs near Cumberland Gap in Kentucky. He had been a lieutenant and aide-de-camp to Confederate General Felix Zollicoffer, who was killed the same day. Henry was a part of Rutledge's Battery, Company A, First Tennessee Artillery commanded by his uncle, Mary Fogg's brother, Arthur Middleton Rutledge.

Henry Fogg had hoped to marry his cousin Seppie, daughter of Henry Adolphus Rutledge. His thoughts of death prompted the writing of a will in August 1861, in which he mentions his cousin Seppie:

> I Henry M. R. Fogg being engaged in Military service, and conscious of the uncertainty of my life, do constitute this my last will and testament as follows towit; I devise to Michael Vaughn, and George P. Bradford my best friends, my block of stock houses in Nashville, Tennessee, on the East side of College Street, South of Church Street, and an undivided interest of one half in a block of offices on Cherry Street, owned in common with said M. Vaughn in trust for the payment of all my just debts, and said realty is hereby charged with the payment of all my debts, and the surplus of said property I hereby bequeath to my father and mother, and to the survivors of them during life, and at their death then to be divided equally between my cousins Arthur M. Rutledge, Jr., and Septima Rutledge, and Emma Fredericka Rutledge—the last being like my own Sister . . . . the object being to give my dear father and mother, to whom I owe more than I can ever repay, full benefit of the corpus of this surplus, as well as of its profits.
>
> I give and bequeath my whole personal estate, consisting chiefly of rent notes, Nashville & Chattanooga R. Road Stock and Books; to my beloved father. To my cousin Septima Rutledge, I give my "Solitaire" diamond ring in the small mahogany box deposited in the Planters Bank. To my Uncle Arthur I give the Seal once belonging to my great grandfather Edward Rutledge, deposited in the same box. To my beloved mother I give my diamond breast pin, and whatever other little valuables I may have. Whatever my dear grandmother intended for me in her will, I wish, if possible, that my cousins Lise, Emma Fredericka & Seppie Rutledge should have the benefit of equally, after my parents death.
>
> I hereby nominate and appoint my father and M. Vaughn and George P. Bradford Executors of this my last Will and Testament, it is my desire that letters testamentary be issued to them without security. Executed and published at Knoxville, Tennessee this 27th day of August 1861.
>
>   H.M.R. Fogg
>
> Witness
>
> W. B. Reese
>
> John L. Brown

**Above detail:
Palmetto Tree
on
Rutledge
Tombstone.**

Photos by Jim Wheeler

**Tombstone of Septima and Henry Rutledge
(side not shown Arthur Middleton Rutledge).**

Photo—Jim Wheeler

Rutledge Plot, Old City Cemetery, Nashville, Tennessee.

The agony of burying a third child for Mary and Francis Fogg must have been a vivid portrait indicative of the pain and sorrow that war brought to families. How bleak that January day must have been for Septima; how cold the realization that death had swept away Henry's namesake; how soon, only a month, would all of Nashville be occupied by the very enemy that had sent Henry Fogg's lifeless form home, there to be placed in the City Cemetery along with his brother, sister, grandfather, and cousin Alice Izard Rutledge. Alice had died August 27, 1854, at age sixteen, while living with the Foggs. The once active, thriving Fogg home at Spring and High across from Christ Episcopal Church, was now the quiet, diminished, residence of Mary, Francis, and their remaining ward, Emma Fredericka Rutledge.

Mary Fogg was truly a remarkable woman. She was known as the "mother of Christ Church," and worked tirelessly throughout the war with Minna and Septima for the Soldiers' Relief Society, the Parish Aid and Sewing Society of the church, and the Ladies' Hospital and Clothing Association, which cared for the soldiers of Tennessee.

She wrote seven books in her lifetime—quite an unusual feat for a woman of that day. They were: *A Biblical View of Church Catechism, Sunday School Teaching, Poems, A Mother's Legacy, The Broken Harp, Mary Ashton* (a novel), and an amazing and accurate textbook entitled *Barrington's Elements of Natural Science.* The first six were published by the Methodist Publishing House and the last by Graves, Marks, and Company.

Henrietta Rutledge and her husband Frederick were buried in the churchyard of St. John in the Wilderness Episcopal Church, Flat Rock, North Carolina. Frederick Rutledge, who lived to be eighty-four years old, never remarried. Of the three children belonging to Henrietta and Frederick who were sent to Septima and Mary Fogg in Nashville, Alice Izard died at age sixteen; Emma Fredericka married William B. Reese, a law instructor at Vanderbilt University; all three are buried in Nashville's Old City Cemetery. Henrietta and Frederick's son, Henry Middleton Rutledge, who became the youngest colonel in the Confederacy, is buried with his parents in Flat Rock. He was the father of Archibald Rutledge, Poet Laureate

Photo—Jim Wheeler

East flanker of Rose Hill which remains at the corner of Rutledge and Lea streets, Nashville, Tennessee.

of South Carolina. The Rutledge plantation, Hampton, on the South
Santee, now belongs to the state of South Carolina, and restoration
is in progress.

Of the three Rutledge children raised at Hampton following
Henrietta's death, Elizabeth Pinckney and Edward are buried in
Flat Rock. Sarah Henrietta became the wife of the Reverend
Charles Cotesworth Pinckney, who served as Rector for St. John
in the Wilderness Parish from 1843-1863. Piedmont, their home in
Flat Rock, was built in 1846. It was a two-story structure with
twenty-two inch stone walls. They are buried at Magnolia Cemetery
Charleston, South Carolina.

Emma Blake died at The Meadows in April of 1853 at the age
of forty-two and is buried at Flat Rock near her sister Henrietta.
Her son Henry Middleton Rutledge Blake died in April, 1856, at
age five. His tombstone, at St. John in the Wilderness churchyard,
bears the inscription, "Is it well with the child? and she answered,
it is well." Daniel Blake raised the remaining five children at The
Meadows and later married Helen Elizabeth Craig of New York,
by whom he had three more children. He lived to be seventy years
old.

It was in 1857 at The Meadows in Fletcher, North Carolina,
that Daniel Blake and his second wife met with a group of wealthy
low-country planters from the community, to organize Calvary
Episcopal Church. There was a great need for a place of worship
closer to the homes of the residents. St. John in the Wilderness was
a day's journey round trip from Fletcher. Those who had become
year-round citizens made plans that evening at The Meadows to
erect a church and, before the dinner meeting had ended, Daniel
Blake agreed to head the committee for the building fund donations.

Frances Caroline Blake, (Emma's daughter—Septima's granddaughter) known to all those living in and near Fletcher as Miss
Fanny, donated several acres of land in back of Calvary Church and
built a school. She was the instructor for many years to follow and
provided cultural and educational opportunties for the children of
that mountain community, which otherwise would have been lack-
ing. She used a book of poems which her mother had written,
published by Daniel Blake the year after Emma died, as part of her
curriculum. The children she taught never forgot her dark gray eyes,
which commanded their attention and showed them she cared that
they try to excel. The graves of Miss Fanny, Daniel, Helen, and

many other Blakes may be found in the oldest section of the cemetery beside Calvary Church.

Henry Adolphus and Caroline Rutledge moved back to Nashville from Alabama, in 1850, to be with Septima. Their daughters, Emma and Seppie, remained in Talladega to finish their school year at Talladega Female Academy. A visitor to the class commencement that spring, West Point Cadet John Horace Forney, fell in love with fourteen-year-old Seppie. She and Emma joined their parents in Nashville, living at Rose Hill, the home of their grandmother, for the next four years. It was during that time that Seppie and her first cousin, Henry Fogg, grew to love each other very much. He showered her with gifts while he was away from America on the "Grand Tour" of Europe, Egypt, and the Middle East with Randal McGavock in 1851-52. Henry Fogg sent home paintings, small sculptured treasures, and sheet music for the pianoforte which he secured along the way for his cousin Seppie. Her classical musical talent was a delight to him, and her Rutledge gray eyes captivated his thoughts.

By 1853, Henry Adolphus had been given part of his father's land grants and had purchased adjoining lands totaling 1,400 acres. It was described as "a certan tract or parcel of land lying in the 7th Civil District in the county of Marion and State of Tennessee on the Southeast side of Sequatchee river about two and a half miles from Jasper." Seppie and her father named this plantation Woodlands. There Seppie spent her days reading, writing poetry, playing her guitar or piano, and riding her favorite horse through the surrounding forest. On July 7, 1853, soon after they moved to Woodlands, Seppie's sister, Emma, married Edwin Turner, a wealthy Alabama planter, and returned to Talladega County to live. Seppie was devoted to her sister and became melancholy at times in her lonely but isolated surroundings.

Mystery still encircles the love Seppie and Henry Fogg shared—none of the family members know why they never married—they

Courtesy—
General John H. Forney,
Historical Society
Photo Designers, Gadsden, Ala.

General John H. Forney, C.S.A. (1829-1902).

only know that it was not until after her cousin Henry's death at the Battle of Fishing Creek that Seppie consented to marry Major General John H. Forney.

In June of 1862, Henry Adolphus Rutledge was captured at Woodlands by Union forces and his brother-in-law, Francis Fogg, arranged for his release. In October 1862, upon his return home, he sold Woodlands and then sent his wife Caroline and daughter Seppie to stay with Emma at the Turner Plantation in Talladega County. It was there General Forney, home on furlough, asked the one he had loved for thirteen years, to be his bride. They were married February 5, 1863, at the home of her sister in a beautiful military ceremony. Emma Rutledge Turner died November 28, 1863, just nine months after Seppie's wedding.

On December 7, 1863, Henry Adolphus and Caroline Bell bought a plantation in Silver Run, Alabama. This plantation, which consisted of a dwelling house, large smoke house, many slave cabins, a cotton gin, and five hundred acres of land, was purchased with Confederate money derived from the sale of Woodlands.

Conditions were desperate at times for all those affected by the war. Seppie's journal reflects the sad memories of her sister Emma and her cousin Henry Fogg. She yearned for security for herself, and her parents, and expressed loneliness when separated from General Forney. Seppie had tried to remain with her husband, traveling with him to Mississippi, only to return to her parents at Silver Run in 1864. There the "Bride of Vicksburg" mourned the past and the impending fall of the Confederacy.

Henry Adolphus and his son-in-law, Gen. John H. Forney, were instrumental in the founding of "The Polytechnique" in the General's home town of Jacksonville, Alabama. The General taught military tactics, mathematics, history and debating, while Henry Adolphus taught the languages and other subjects in the curriculum. All the students wore Confederate gray uniforms with brass buttons. This school was the forerunner of Jacksonville State University.

Henry Adolphus and Caroline later lived with the Forneys near Selma, Alabama, where Henry died September 23, 1883. Caroline, his wife, died December 23, 1878. They were both buried in Live Oak Cemetery in Selma.

Courtesy—Mary Stevenson Poling and Eleanor Stevenson Rutledge

General John H. Forney and wife "Seppie" Rutledge Forney. Grandchildren, left to right—Kathleen Theresa Daugette (Carson), John McLaughlin Forney, Palmer Daugette (Calvert), John Forney Stevenson, Horace Lee Stevenson, Caroline Forney (Pain).

Arthur Middleton Rutledge, youngest surviving child of Septima and Henry Rutledge, married Eliza "Light" Underwood, daughter of Judge Joseph Rogers and Elizabeth Trotter Underwood of Kentucky on November 4, 1851. They made their home at Chilhowee in Franklin County, Tennessee, where Arthur continued to manage the mills and became a successful planter.

They had four children; Elizabeth Underwood born August 29, 1852, Emma Blake born March 29, 1854, Arthur Middleton, Jr., born November 4, 1855, and Joseph Underwood Huger born May 3, 1859.

Early in the 1850s a slave belonging to Arthur was murdered by a slave belonging to a family named Rowe. In settlement for the loss, a large, valuable, tract of land was deeded to Arthur M. Rutledge. On this 410 acre tract was located "Rowe's Cabin" which was the stagecoach stop on the intersecting routes between Nashville, Tennessee, and Atlanta, Georgia, and between Virginia and

Courtesy—Middleton Place Foundation

Pass issued to "Light" Rutledge by Abraham Lincoln.

Mississippi. These were the two main lines of stagecoach and wagon travel for Middle Tennessee and was later called the "Tremlett Spring" site.

This land was given for the building of the University of the South at Sewanee, Tennessee, by Arthur in 1857. The idea for the school came from James Hervey Otey, first Episcopal Bishop of Tennessee. He inspired Louisiana Bishop Leonidas Polk to pattern a school after Oxford University in England. Bishop Polk circulated a letter calling for support from every Southern Diocese. The Sewanee Mining Company donated five thousand acres with private citizens donating the remainder, the largest gift coming from Arthur M. Rutledge.

Francis B. Fogg obtained the charter for the University, was first registrar, and a lay trustee for many years. Arthur was also a trustee, along with his brother-in-law. Arthur's son Joseph died at Sewanee while in school August 30, 1876. That same year Arthur, Jr., was valedictorian of the University's third graduating class.

The pink marble cornerstone, quarried near the head waters of the Elk River, required thirty-two oxen to transport it to the brow of the Cumberland Plateau. The ceremonies, October 10, 1860, for the laying of the cornerstone were elaborate. Between four and five thousand people thronged to the mountainside gala. Arthur Rutledge was marshall of the day and arranged the details of the program. There was a procession of laymen, a brass band, followed by the clergy carrying a large cross, and ending with the bishops from eight southern states dressed in full vestment.

There was a shed constructed just for the occasion, bountiful food catered from Nashville, speeches in abundance, and great throngs of people who came on foot, horseback, and in wagons and carriages of every sort. There were two special trains from Nashville transporting four hundred leading clergy and laity, two bands of music, plus all necessary provisions for food and bedding for five thousand people. This was a strange sight indeed for the mountain folk who must have marveled at such extravagant proceedings just to ask God's blessing on a future school.

Even stranger was the fate of that beautiful, giant, ruddy, polished native marble. In July of 1863 a Union regiment, encamped on the University grounds, blew the great cornerstone into small pieces—just the right size for souveniers to carry home. Franklin County was desecrated, stripped of all resources by Union Generals

Buell, Rosecrans, and even Sherman as late as the winter of 1863-64. The University of the South was rebuilt, and Major Arthur Middleton Rutledge lived there following the war. His wife "Light" died May 2, 1865, just eight days before President Andrew Johnson declared an end to the War Between the States. She is buried in Fairview Cemetery, Bowling Green, Kentucky. Arthur married Marie Adams of Boston on April 25, 1875, and died at Sewanee June 17, 1876. He is buried with his parents in Nashville's Old City Cemetery. His widow remained at Sewanee for some years where she ran a "student hall" or dormitory. She died in Washington, D. C., May 22, 1887. Elizabeth married Henry Edward Young and Emma married Henry Augustus Middleton Smith, both of Charleston. Their brother, Arthur, Jr., married Rosalie Winston and they resided in Kentucky.

Courtesy—Tennessee Historical Society

Officers of Rutledge's Battery
Center standing—Arthur Middleton Rutledge (1817-1876)

Epilogue

At the time of the War Between the States, Middleton Place was owned by Williams Middleton, son of Henry and Mary Helen Hering Middleton. Williams and his wife Susan Pringle Smith were forced to flee their home with the advance of Union forces. The house itself was destroyed by fire February 22, 1865, and crumbled during the earthquake in 1886. Only the south flanker remained. The family returned and lived there during the years of the Restoration.

Elizabeth Middleton, daughter of Williams and Susan, married John Julius Heyward in 1881 and subsequently left Middleton Place to her cousin John Julius Pringle Smith. His grandfather, John Julius Pringle Smith, married Elizabeth, who was a granddaughter of Thomas Middleton (brother of Arthur Middleton, the signer). They had a son Henry Augustus Middleton Smith who married Emma Blake Rutledge (daughter of Arthur Middleton Rutledge and granddaughter of Septima and Henry). Their son John Julius Pringle Smith and his wife Heningham Lyons Ellett began restoration on Middleton Place in 1916. They were the grandparents of Charles H. P. Duell, present-day owner of the gardens. The south flanker is under the aegis of the Middleton Place Foundation. Located on Highway 61, fourteen miles northwest of Charleston, Middleton Place House and Gardens re-creates for visitors a vivid example of a working plantation or country seat.

Middleton Place is a Registered National Historic Landmark. The landscaped gardens are the oldest in America. It was there that André Michaux planted four of the first camellias in the New World nearly two centuries ago.

Among the beautiful furnishings and family heirlooms hangs the portrait of Septima, painted by Edward Marchant in 1825. It is noteworthy that Middleton Place returned to its former glory through the efforts of her great-grandson.

We are grateful to Middleton Place Foundation director Sarah Lytle and her staff for their acceptance of us and our project, their willingness to answer questions and to allow us access to their archives. Cheves Leland was particularly helpful in locating data

Courtesy—Charles H. P. Duell
Photo—R. Alan Powell

**Emma Blake Rutledge Smith
(1854-1940)**

Courtesy—Charles H. P. Duell
Photo—R. Alan Powell

**Judge Henry Augustus
Middleton Smith
(1853-1924)**

Courtesy—Middleton Place Foundation

**Tomb of Arthur Middleton (died January 1, 1787) who is buried
with his mother, his son Henry, his grandson Williams, and his
great-granddaughter Elizabeth.**

concerning the Middletons. Barbara Smith, as founding editor of the *Middleton Place Notebook,* kept us informed as to discoveries concerning both the Middleton and Rutledge families. She very graciously shared her time and the information on remaining artifacts which belonged to Septima and Henry. Barbara's husband Benjamin Bosworth Smith is the great-grandson of Emma Fredericka "Minna" Rutledge Reese (daughter of Frederick and Henrietta Rutledge). Minna's granddaughter Katherine Felder Stewart assisted us greatly with her contribution of information concerning Septima. She cherished conversations with her grandmother Minna and shared her knowledge of the family with us.

The William Blake home on East Bay, which was leased by Mary Izard Middleton, has been restored for use by the Citizens and Southern National Bank in Charleston. The Edward Rutledge home at 117 Broad Street is the private residence of Mr. and Mrs. Joseph P. Griffith. They have restored the house, which was used for a Roman Catholic school for many years, capturing much of its original grandeur. Directly across Broad Street is the John Rutledge home. It now serves as offices for several law firms.

St. Philip's, St. Michael's, St. Andrew's, Christ Church Parish, St. James Santee, and St. James Goosecreek Episcopal churches may be visited in the Charleston area. They and their churchyards, along with Magnolia cemetery and places of private burial, are present-day reminders of the lives depicted within this biography.

Cedar Grove, Canteys, Jenys, Janesse, the Rutledge home at Federal Green and Front (present day Calhoun and East Bay) are no longer standing, but much of old "Charles Town" remains to give credence to the past.

Of particular help with the Charleston research was Elise Pinckney (great-granddaughter of Frederick and Henrietta Rutledge). She is the present editor of the South Carolina Historical Magazine. Our conversations and correspondence with her supplied important links concerning both Charleston and Flat Rock, North Carolina.

The summer resort at Flat Rock, still known by many as the "Little Charleston of the Mountains," is a viable year-round community today. St. John in the Wilderness Episcopal Church, on Highway 25 southwest of Hendersonville, holds regular services and is open for visitors.

The Old Mill is located just off Highway 25 on Earl's Creek. There the sturdy, functional, "Flat Rock Chair" was developed. Sofas and rockers were also made in the same style. All three varieties are now collector's items. The Old Mill has become a popular and attractive motel complex owned and operated by the Manus family.

Many of the Flat Rock estates mentioned in this biography remain as private residences. The Rutledge cottage, owned by Mr. and Mrs. Alexander Schenck, was once the home of Elizabeth and Sarah Henrietta Rutledge (daughters of Frederick and Henrietta Rutledge). Mr. Schenck was a valuable contact for us and helped with many details about the Flat Rock area and its residents.

Of particular importance was the location of the Meadows in nearby Fletcher, North Carolina. Mr. Schenck arranged for us to interview the owner, William T. Justice. We met Mr. Justice at his exclusive William and Mary clothing store on Highway 25, north of Hendersonville. We envisioned Emma and Daniel Blake journeying home on Sundays from services at St. John in the Wilderness and the eventual necessity of building a place of worship in Fletcher. Mr. Justice toured the Blake house and grounds with us and pointed out many facts necessary to our story. At that time a portion of the old Murray Inn was still standing near the side entrance of the Meadows. Of interest were the giant boxwoods that were brought from England for Daniel Blake. They are now the largest in the eastern United States and possibly in the entire country. There is room to walk inside the enormous shrubs, with several feet of head room to spare.

Mr. Justice said he would never forget our excitement over the magnificent old house and grounds. He was also particularly touched at our reaction to the discovery of so many of our "family" names on the tombstones in the Calvary Episcopal churchyard.

Co-owners William Justice and John C. Youngblood, Sr., have subsequently sold the Meadows to Kellwood Company of Asheville, North Carolina. They plan to use the home as an executive guest house, once construction of their plant is completed.

Frederick and Henrietta Rutledge divided their time between Western Carolina and their plantation near Charleston. In 1937 their grandson, Archibald Rutledge, returned to Hampton plantation where he lovingly worked to restore and care for his ancestral home. In 1951 his son, Archibald, Jr., married Eleanor Stevenson Parker (granddaughter of Septima Sexta Middleton "Seppie" Rutledge Forney). Archibald, Arch, and Eleanor lived at Hampton, near the King's Highway, and for more than twenty years welcomed visitors to the stately mansion north of Charleston off U. S. 17.

Archibald Rutledge, who was Poet Laureate of South Carolina, did much of his writing there by the South Santee River. His books, particularly *Home by the River* and *My Colonel and His Lady,* capture forever the unique spirit of Hampton. The property is now owned by the state of South Carolina. Both Archibald and his son Arch are buried there.

Eleanor Rutledge now lives in Jacksonville, Alabama where General John H. Forney and his wife Seppie Rutledge once made their home. Eleanor made available valuable details concerning two children of Septima and Henry; Eleanor's own ancestor, Henry Adolphus Rutledge, and her husband's great-grandmother, Henrietta Middleton Rutledge Rutledge. We are truly indebted to this charming gracious lady for her assistance. She and her sister, Mary Abernathy Stevenson Poling, delighted us with each remembrance of vital conversations with their "Grandmother Forney." We were immediately encircled by warmth and enthusiasm from the very first visit with our Alabama "family of the heart." Seppie's grandchildren welcomed us and made each and every research trip a special occasion. Horace Lee and Sarah Katherine Stevenson shared a marvelous collection of genealogical data and together with Horace Lee's sisters, Eleanor and Mary, gave us many stories told them by their mother, Sabina Swope Morgan Forney Stevenson. Sabina and her sisters Emma Forney, Mary Caroline Forney, and Annie Rowan Forney Daugette were dedicated in their preservation of Seppie's family treasures.

The Daugette home, the Magnolias, became our Alabama headquarters while we gathered material for this biography. Presently owned by the Estate of Annie Rowan Forney Daugette, the Magnolias is the residence of her daughter, Kathleen Daugette Carson, and is adjacent to the home of another daughter, Palmer Daugette Calvert, and her husband, Dr. William J. Calvert, Jr. While staying at the Magnolias, we enjoyed the privacy of our own suite on the second floor and were given complete access to their collection of rare volumes, pictures, scrapbooks, journals, and unpublished manuscripts. Our every need was cared for by Lenora Carr Murphree during the process of transcribing and compiling necessary data. Maurice Johnson assured our welcome and along with Mrs. Murphree reinforced what we had already come to realize—that Septima's strength of character had made the successful transition to the present generations as evidenced by descendants like Sabina Stevenson and Annie Daugette.

An essential element, in the reconstruction of Septima's story, was the location of Chilhowee in Middle Tennessee. Copies of original Revolutionary War grants, county deeds, even the wording of several wills had to be scrutinized for the necessary information.

In the spring of 1978, we met Dr. Edward McCrady while we were in Charleston. We arranged an interview with him and his wife, Edith, the following June at their home in Sewanee, Tennessee. Dr. McCrady, retired vice-chancellor of the University of the South, shared his knowledge of the property given to the university by Septima and Henry's son Arthur Middleton Rutledge. This tract of 410 acres, which Arthur donated to the school, was located at the crossroads of the stage routes from Nashville to Atlanta and from Virginia to Mississippi. The gymnasium and the athletic fields are now on part of this tract. Rutledge Point, one of the more popular views, was named for Arthur who was a trustee of the University in 1858. Francis Fogg secured the school's charter and was the first registrar.

Dr. McCrady gave us directions down the mountain toward Nashville, past the crossroads at Alto (once called Hawkersville), along what had been a stagecoach road to the old Rutledge ford across the Elk River. With great anticipation we followed Dr. McCrady's directions. As we left Sewanee we were aware of the magnificent Cumberland Plateau as it extended for miles to our right. Deeper into the valley we approached an unmarked narrow bridge. Somehow we knew the steep rise ahead must surely have been the best location for a plantation house—maybe, just maybe, Chilhowee. We slowed to look at the swifly flowing stream of water beneath the bridge—then, not daring to be too optimistic, we approached the crest of the hill. There was a man on a tractor observing us with some curiosity. We said hello and then very quickly asked if he knew where there might have been an old Rutledge house. A steady smile crossed his face as he pointed to our left and said without hesitation that it had stood back there in his family's corn field. With incredible excitement and belated introductions we left the automobile parked in front of a farm house and followed the local postman, Mr. Albert Sherrill, some few hundred yards until we were standing as close as possible to the foundation site of Chilhowee itself. Recovering enough composure to ask questions about the house was not easy. The view alone was breathtaking without the added thrill of discovering the trail's end that had greeted the Rutledge cavalcade from Charleston one hundred and sixty-two years before. We left reluctantly, knowing we would return. We were anxious to interview Albert Sherrill's father Arthur, as he was the only one left in the area who remembered the house.

Albert told us to turn right at the church and go about one-half mile to see "Dad." The church—we hadn't even noticed the small brick structure across the way—was the "Rutledge Hill Community Church." Unforgettable moments were multiplying—and then we met Mr. Arthur Sherrill. His kind face crinkled with a grin we would always remember. It was amazing to him that two ladies from Nashville could possibly be so curious about the Rutledge house. He

showed us the deeds signed in 1889 by the surviving children
of Arthur Middleton Rutledge and gave us many details about
Chilhowee.

On subsequent trips to see Mr. Sherrill he took us in his truck
to see the grove of trees where the slaves were buried, the hand dug
mill race, the spring and cave between the plantation site and the
river, and patiently answered question after question.

In June of 1979, we stopped to see Mr. Sherrill on the way home
from a research trip to Alabama. He sat in the swing on the front
porch and listened to the portions of our manuscript which described
Chilhowee. His eyes were moist as he said softly, "It sounds to me
like you must have been right there." Mr. Arthur Sherrill died
August 1, 1979, and is buried in the churchyard on Rutledge Hill.
We are grateful to him for recreating Chilhowee, and we are happy
he was pleased with what was written about his land. We deeply
appreciate the kindness shown us by him and his loved ones. Mr.
Sherrill has become part of our "family of the heart," and we miss
him.

Nashville, Tennessee has entered a third century; only the east
flanker of Rose Hill remains at the corner of Rutledge and Lea
streets and is now subdivided into apartments; restoration efforts for
Rutledge Hill have received much recent publicity; the Rutledge
plot in the Old City Cemetery on Fourth Avenue South and Oak
Street is indicated by a bronze marker; Christ Episcopal Church
moved its location to the corner of Broad and Ninth Avenue North,
holding the first service in the new sanctuary on Sunday, December
16, 1894—Christ Church has sponsored eighteen missions, with
twelve of these still active—"the Mother Church" recently celebrated one hundred fifty years in Nashville; Hume-Fogg High
School, also on Broad Street, combines the names of two citizens
instrumental in the founding of public education in the city—educa-
tor William C. Hume and Francis B. Fogg, first president of the
Board of Education; the Fogg home, that once stood at present day
Sixth and Church, has been replaced by the Watkins Institute building; the House of Industry became the home of the Nashville
Y.W.C.A. on Seventh until their recent move to Woodmont Boule-

vard; the Protestant Orphan Asylum no longer stands near Eighth Avenue South—its purpose now being carried on by denominational children's homes in other parts of the city; Andrew Jackson's home, the Hermitage, located about twelve miles east of Nashville, off I-40, on Lebanon Road is open to visitors year round as is Tulip Grove, the nearby home of Jackson's nephew Andrew Jackson Donelson; streets in south Nashville bear the names Middleton, Rutledge, and Fogg and portions of the old University of Nashville remain on what is called "Historic Rutledge Hill."

The grandchildren of Septima and Henry Rutledge sold most of the land left to them due to resettlement following the war. Yet they and the generations that followed left schools, universities, charitable institutions, and churches as living monuments to the cultural pioneering spirit that was their legacy.

In 1884 Henry Drummond, in his essay *The Greatest Thing In The World,* reiterated with the apostle Paul that the "supreme good," which alone is eternal and abiding, is Love. In reference to that, he said, "What we are stretches past what we do, beyond what we possess."

It was in becoming what they were, within their chosen exile that Septima and Henry, indeed all the generations that followed Arthur Middleton and Edward Rutledge through them, brought a noble dream into reality. Promises fulfilled—destinies secured—symbols of the past forged by rugged principle and determination into a new society—an irreplaceable model for the future.

Resources

Historical societies, libraries, archives, foundations, private collections, and church registries all contain invaluable primary source material. Yet without the assistance of dedicated personnel, avid local historians, and those descendants and family members gracious enough to share their homes, their memories, and themselves the information for this biography would not have been complete. Grateful acknowledgement is given to the following:

Alabama
Gadsden;
Colonel Clarence W. Daugette, Jr.
Florence Throckmorton Daugette
Anne Daugette Renfrow
Raymond R. Renfrow, Jr.
  Anne Clare Renfrow
  Rosalie Florence Renfrow
Burt Daugette Lowe
Lynn Lowe
Clarence W. Daugette, III
Forney Rutledge Daugette, Jr.
Ken Dempsey
Maurice Johnson
Marcella Lawley
Paul Meloun
Jacksonville;
The Forney-Stevenson Home
  Mary Abernathy Stevenson Poling
  Eleanor Stevenson Rutledge
General John H. Forney Historical
  Society
General John H. Forney Chapter,
  United Daughters of the
  Confederacy
Jacksonville Heritage Association
The Magnolias
  Kathleen Daugette Carson
  Lenora Carr Murphree
St. Luke's Episcopal Church
Palmer Daugette Calvert
Dr. William J. Calvert, Jr.
Horace Lee Stevenson
Sarah Katherine Stevenson

District of Columbia
Washington;
Library of Congress
National Archives
  Audio Visual Department
  Jim Moore
  Tom Oglesby
Edward Thomas Dority

Florida
Pensacola;
Historic Pensacola Preservation
    Board
    Linda V. Ellsworth
St. Augustine;
    St. Augustine Historical Society

Georgia
Atlanta;
  J. C. Harris, Jr.
Darien;
  Miss Bessie Lewis
Spring Place;
The Vann House
  Mr. and Mrs. James E. Hall
  Department of Natural Resources–
  Parks and Historic Sites Division
St. Simons Island;
Museum of Coastal History
  Anita Fulton
  Mildred Nix Huie

Kentucky
Louisville;
The Filson Club
  Nellie Watson

New York
Saratoga Springs;
Office of City Historian
  Mrs. Michael E. Sweeney

North Carolina
Flat Rock;
Historic Flat Rock, Inc.
  John Wesley Jones
  Mrs. Robert E. Mason
The Old Mill
  Mr. & Mrs. Manus
Rutledge Cottage
  Mr. & Mrs. Alexander Schenck
St. John in the Wilderness Episcopal
    Church
  Reginald C. FitzSimons
  The Rev. Walter D. Roberts
  Mr. & Mrs. William I. Van Gelder
Frank L. FitzSimons
Elinor Gorham
Elizabeth Lowndes
Clarence Peace
Elise Pinckney
Fletcher;
Calvary Episcopal Church
  The Rev. Mark Jenkins
The Meadows
  William T. Justice
  John C. Youngblood, Sr.
  Kellwood Company
  Jack R. Howerton
  Mr. & Mrs. Hal Smith
Meadowview
  Mr. & Mrs. Edwin H. Tillman
Hendersonville;
Baker-Barber Collection
  Jody Barber
  Fenno VanderVeen
The Times-News
  Lucile S. Ray

Pennsylvania
Philadelphia;
Pennsylvania Historical Society
  James E. Mooney
  Lucy L. Hrivnak
  Diane Telian

South Carolina
Camden;
  Mrs. Frederick Reeves Rutledge
Charleston;

William Blake House
  Citizens and Southern National
    Bank
Middleton Place Foundation
  Charles H. P. Duell
  Sarah Lytle
  Cheves Leland
  Barbara Smith
  Ellen Clark
  Barbara Doyle
  R. Alan Powell
  Martha Deweese
Edward Rutledge House
  Mr. & Mrs. Joseph P. Griffith
St. Philip's Episcopal Church
    Vestrymen
  Dr. Edward McCrady
South Carolina Historical Society
  Gene Waddell
  Elise Pinckney
  Sallie Doscher
Trident Chamber of Commerce
Kathryn Felder Stewart
Columbia;
State House of South Carolina
South Carolina State Library and
    Archives
University of South Carolina
  South Caroliniana Library
  Les Inabinett
  Rhett Hamiter
  Marlene T. Sipes

Tennessee
Murfreesboro;
Oaklands
  Rick Harrell
Nashville;
Christ Episcopal Church Archives
  Laura Drake
Old City Cemetery
  Naomi Levia
  Leslie Paine
  Edythe Rucker Whitley
The Hermitage
  Ladies' Hermitage Association
  Mrs. Allen Steele
  Edith Thornton
  Millye McGehee
The Papers of Andrew Jackson
  Charles F. Bryan, Jr.

Sharon Macpherson
Historic Nashville, Inc.
Metropolitan Nashville Historical
  Commission
Public Library of Nashville and
  Davidson County
  Ben West Library
  Dorothy Dale
  Nashville Room
  Mary Glenn Hearne
  Hershel G. Payne
  Elsie Kolar
  Thompson Lane Branch
Tennessee Historical Commission
  Barbara Church
Tennessee Historical Society
  James A. Hoobler
Tennessee State Library and Archives
  Sara Harwell
  John Thweatt
Vanderbilt University Medical
  Library
  Special Collections Division

Mary Teloh
Young Women's Christian
  Association
  Dena Fredebeil
  Frances Cate Grigsby
  Mrs. Arthur Tatum
Petersburg;
  Mrs. H. B. Whitaker
  Mark Whitaker
Rutledge Hill Community;
  Albert Sherrill
  Arthur Sherrill
Sewanee;
University of the South
  Dr. & Mrs. Edward McCrady
  Trudy Mignery
Winchester;
Franklin County Historical Society
  Jail Museum
  Maye Gattis
Franklin County Library and
  Archives
  Nelle Hanson

Selected Bibliography

Abernethy, Thomas Perkins. *From Frontier to Plantation in Tennessee: A Study in Frontier Democracy.* Chapel Hill: The University of North Carolina Press, 1932.

Arnow, Harriette Simpson. *Flowering of the Cumberland.* New York: The Macmillan Company, 1963.

_____. *Seedtime on the Cumberland.* New York: The Macmillan Company, 1960.

Ball, William Watts. *The State That Forgot: South Carolina's Surrender to Democracy.* Indianapolis: The Bobbs-Merrill Company, 1932.

Bassett, John Spencer, Ph.D. (ed.). *Correspondence of Andrew Jackson.* Vol. III, *1820-1828.* Washington, D.C.: Carnegie Institution, 1933.

Becker, Stephen (trans.). *Diary of My Travels in America,* by Louis-Philippe, King of France, 1830-1848. New York: Delacorte Press, 1977.

Brandau, Roberta Sewell, (ed.). *History of Homes and Gardens, of Tennessee.* Nashville: Parthenon Press, 1936.

Burt, Jesse C. *Nashville: Its Life and Times.* Nashville: Tennessee Book Company, 1959.

Cheves, Langdon, Esq. "Middleton of South Carolina." Vol. I, South Carolina Historical and Genealogical Magazine, 1900.

Clayton, W. W. *The History of Davidson County, Tennessee.* 1880. Reprint. Nashville: Charles Elder, 1971.

Coke, Fletch. *Christ Church.* Nashville: Williams Printing Company, 1979.

Crabb, Alfred Leland. *Nashville: Personality of a City.* Indianapolis-New York: The Bobbs-Merrill Co., Inc., 1960.

Crane, Sophie, and Paul Crane. *Tennessee Taproots.* Old Hickory: Earle-Shields, 1976.

Crawford, Lee Forney. *Forney Forever.* Birmingham: Commercial Printing Co., 1967.

Davidson, Donald. *The Tennessee, Frontier to Secession,* Rivers of America Series, Vol. 1. New York: Rinehart & Co., 1946.

_____. *The Tennessee, The New River: Civil War to TVA,* Rivers of America Series, Vol. 2 New York: Rinehart & Co., 1948.

Davis, Louise Littleton. *Frontier Tales of Tennessee.* Gretna: Pelican Publishing Co., 1976.

_____. *More Tales of Tennessee.* Gretna: Pelican Publishing Co., 1978.

Drummond, Henry. *The Greatest Thing In The World.* London: Collins, n.d.

Dykeman, Wilma. *The French Broad.* Knoxville: University of Tennessee Press, 1966.

Egerton, John. *Nashville: The Faces of Two Centuries (1780-1980).* Nashville: Nashville Magazine, 1979.

Engel, Beth Bland. *The Middleton Family (including Myddelton and Myddleton): records from Wales, England, Barbados, and the southern United States.* Jesup: Press of the Jesup Sentinel, 1972.

Ferris, John C. *Homes for the Homeless or Fourteen Years Among the Orphans.* Nashville: Publishing House of the Methodist Episcopal Church, South, 1890.

Fogg, Mary Middleton Rutledge. *Barrington's Elements of Natural Science comprising Hydrology, Geognosy, Geology, Meteorology, Botany, Zoology, and Anthropology.* Nashville: Graves, Marks & Co., 1858.

————————. *A Biblical View of the Church Catechism in reference to Baptismal Responsibilities: elucidating, by numerous texts of scripture, the doctrines and principles of the Church, with a view to confirmation.* Nashville: Paul & Tavel, 1870.

Fraser, Charles. *A Charleston Sketchbook,* ed. Alice R. Huger Smith. Charleston: Carolina Art Association, 1971.

————————. *Reminiscences of Charleston.* Charleston: Garnier & Company, 1969.

Freeman, Douglas Southall. *George Washington: a Biography.* Vol. 6, *Patriot and President.* New York: C. Scribner's Sons, 1948-1957.

————————. *George Washington: a Biography.* Vol. 7, *First in Peace.* New York: C. Scribner's Sons, 1948-1957.

Gailor, Charlotte, and others. (eds.). *Purple Sewanee.* Sewanee: Association for the Preservation of Tennessee Antiquities, 1961.

Gerson, Noel B. *The Velvet Glove: A Life of Dolly Madison.* Nashville-New York: Thomas Nelson Publishers, 1975.

Goodpasture, A. V., and W. R. Garrett. *History of Tennessee, It's People and Institutions.* Nashville: Brandon Printing Co., 1900.

Goodspeed (ed.) *History of Tennessee from the earliest times to the present; together with an historical and a biographical sketch of Cannon, Coffee, DeKalb, Warren and White Counties.* Chicago and Nashville: Goodspeed, firm, publishers, 1887.

Goodspeed (ed.). *History of Tennessee from the earliest times to the present; together with an historical and a biographical sketch of Giles, Lincoln, Franklin and Moore Counties.* Chicago and Nashville: Goodspeed, firm, publishers, 1886.

Govan, Gilbert E., and James W. Livingood. *The Chattanooga Country 1540-1962: From Tomahawk to TVA.* Chapel Hill: University of North Carolina, 1952. rev. ed. University of Chattanooga, 1963.

Gower, Herschel, and Jack Allen, (eds.). *Pen and Sword, the Life and Journals of Randal W. McGavock*. With a brief biography of Randal W. McGavock by Herschel Gower. Nashville: Tennessee Historical Commission, 1960.

Graham, Eleanor (ed.). *Nashville: A Short History and Selected Buildings*. Nashville: Historical Commission of Metropolitan Nashville-Davidson County, Tennessee, 1974.

Grigsby, Frances Cate. "Mary Middleton Rutledge Fogg," *Seven Women of Nashville: Nashville's Fine Flavor of Feminity*. Nashville: Public Library of Nashville and Davidson County, 1974.

Hale, William Thomas, and Dixon Merritt. *History of Tennessee and Tennesseans*. Chicago: Lewis Publishing Co., 1913.

Jenkins, Mark. *Calvary Church: First 100 Years*. Fletcher: Calvary Episcopal Church, 1959.

Kemble, Frances Anne. *Journal of a Residence On a Georgia Plantation in 1838-1839*. New York: The New American Library, Inc., 1975.

Leach, Frank Willing. *Genealogy of the Signers of the Declaration of Independence: original letters and summaries*. 53 vols. from 1885 to 1916.

——————. Typewritten Copy of original manuscripts. John Calvert and Evelyn R. Dale (eds.). 20 vols., 1927.

Leiding, Harriette Kershaw. *Historic and Romantic Charleston*. Philadelphia: J. B. Lippincott Company, 1931.

Linton, Calvin D., Ph. D. (ed.). *The American Almanac: A Diary of America*. Nashville: Thomas Nelson, Inc., 1977.

Lovell, Caroline Couper. *The Golden Isles of Georgia*. Atlanta: Cherokee Publishing Co., 1970.

MacKellar, William H. *Chuwalee: Chronicles of Franklin County, Tennessee*. Winchester: Franklin County Historical Society, 1973.

Malone, Dumas. *The Story of the Declaration of Independence*. New York: Oxford University Press, 1954.

Marsh, Kenneth, and Blanche Marsh. *Historic Flat Rock: Where The Old South Lingers*. Columbia: R. L. Bryan Company, 1972.

Michael, William. *The Declaration of Independence*. Washington: Government Printing Office, 1904.

Middleton, Alicia Hopton. *Life in Carolina and New England in the Nineteenth Century*. Bristol (R.I.): privately printed, 1929.

Molloy, Robert. *Charleston: A Gracious Heritage*. New York: D. Appleton-Century Company, Inc., 1947.

Moltke-Hansen, David, and Sallie Doscher (eds.). *South Carolina Historical Society Manuscript Guide*. Charleston: South Carolina Historical Society, 1979.

Morris, Eastin. *Tennessee Gazetteer 1834 and Matthew Rhea's Map of the State of Tennessee 1832,* eds. Robert M. McBride and Owen Meredith. Nashville: The Gazetteer Press, 1971.

Owsley, Harriet Chappel, (ed.). *Guide to the Processed Manuscripts of the Tennessee Historical Society.* Nashville: Tennessee Historical Commission, Tennessee State Library and Archives, 1969.

Patton, Sadie Smathers. *The Story of Henderson County.* Spartanburg: The Reprint Company, 1976.

Rankin, Anne (ed.). *Christ Church Nashville: 1829-1929* Nashville: Marshall and Bruce, 1929.

Ravenel, Mrs. St. Julien. *Charleston: The Place and the People.* New York: The MacMillan Co., 1929.

Rhett, Robert Goodwyn. *Charleston: An Epic of Carolina.* Richmond: Garrett and Massie, Incorporated, 1940.

Rutledge, Archibald. *Beauty in the Heart: including Meet Archibald Rutledge* by Frank S. Mead. Westwood: Fleming H. Revell Co., 1953.

——————————. *God's Children.* Indianapolis-New York: The Bobbs-Merrill Company, 1947.

——————————. *Home by the River.* Indianapolis-New York: The Bobbs-Merrill Company, 1941.

——————————. *Life's Extras.* New York-Chicago: Fleming H. Revell Co., 1928.

——————————. *My Colonel and His Lady.* Indianapolis-New York: The Bobbs-Merrill Company, 1937.

——————————. *Peace in the Heart.* Garden City: Doubleday & Company, Inc., 1949.

Rutledge, Sarah. *The Carolina Housewife,* ed. Anna Wells Rutledge. Columbia: University of South Carolina Press, 1979.

Simms, William Gilmore. *The History of South Carolina, from its First European Discovery to its Erection into a Republic.* Redfield, 1860.

Templin, Eleanor. "Franklin County Families: The Remarkable Rutledge Family." *The Franklin County Historical Review.* Vol. VII, 1976.

Thomas, Jane H. *Old Days in Nashville.* 1895-96. Reprint. Nashville: Charles Elder, 1969.

Uhlendorf, Bernhard Alexander. *The Seige of Charleston.* New York: New York Times, 1968.

Walker, Hugh. *Tennessee Tales.* Nashville: Aurora Press, 1971.

Waller, George. *Saratoga: Saga of an Impious Era.* Englewood Cliffs: Prentice Hall, Inc., 1966.

Webber, Mabel L. (ed.). "Dr. John Rutledge and His Descendants." *South Carolina Historical and Genealogical Magazine.* Vol. XXXI, 1930.

Williams, Frances Leigh. *A Founding Family: The Pinckneys of South Carolina.* New York and London: Harcourt Brace Lavanovich, 1978.

Windrow, John E. (ed.). *Peabody and Alfred Leland Crabb: The Story of Peabody as Reflected in Selected Writings of Alfred Leland Crabb.* Nashville: Williams Press, 1977.

Wooldridge, John. *History of Nashville, Tennessee.* 1890. Reprint. Nashville: Charles Elder, 1970.

Index